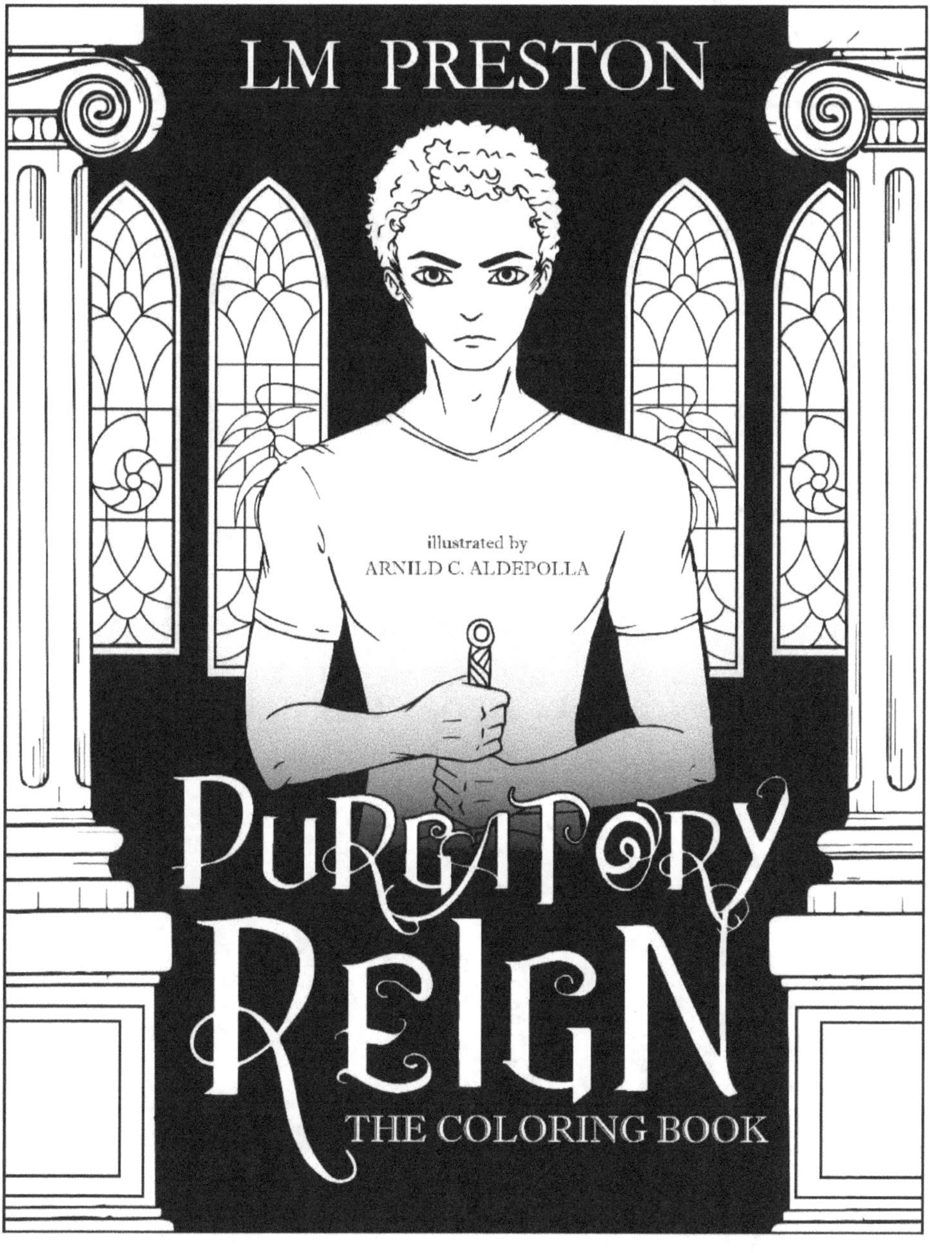

LM PRESTON

illustrated by
ARNILD C. ALDEPOLLA

PURGATORY REIGN
THE COLORING BOOK

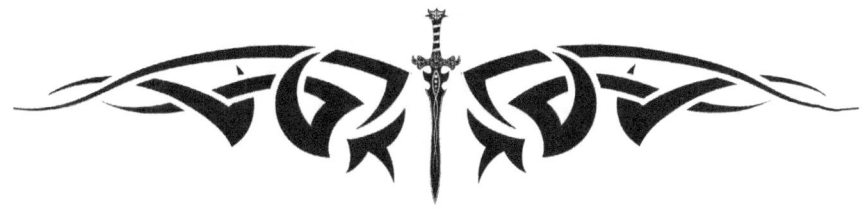

COPYRIGHTS

Reproducing this book without permission from the author or the publisher is an infringement of its copyright. This book is a work of fiction. The names characters, places, and incidents are products of the author's imagination and are not to be construed as real. Any resemblance to any actual events or persons, living or dead, locale or organizations is entirely coincidental.

Copyright © 2018 L.M. Preston.
All rights reserved.
ISBN-13: 978-1719586191

Illustrated by Arnild Aldepolla
Interior design & Formatting by Stephany Wallace. All Rights Reserved.

A Phenomenal One Press publication. Jun, 2018
www.phenomenalonepress.com

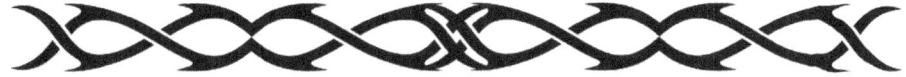

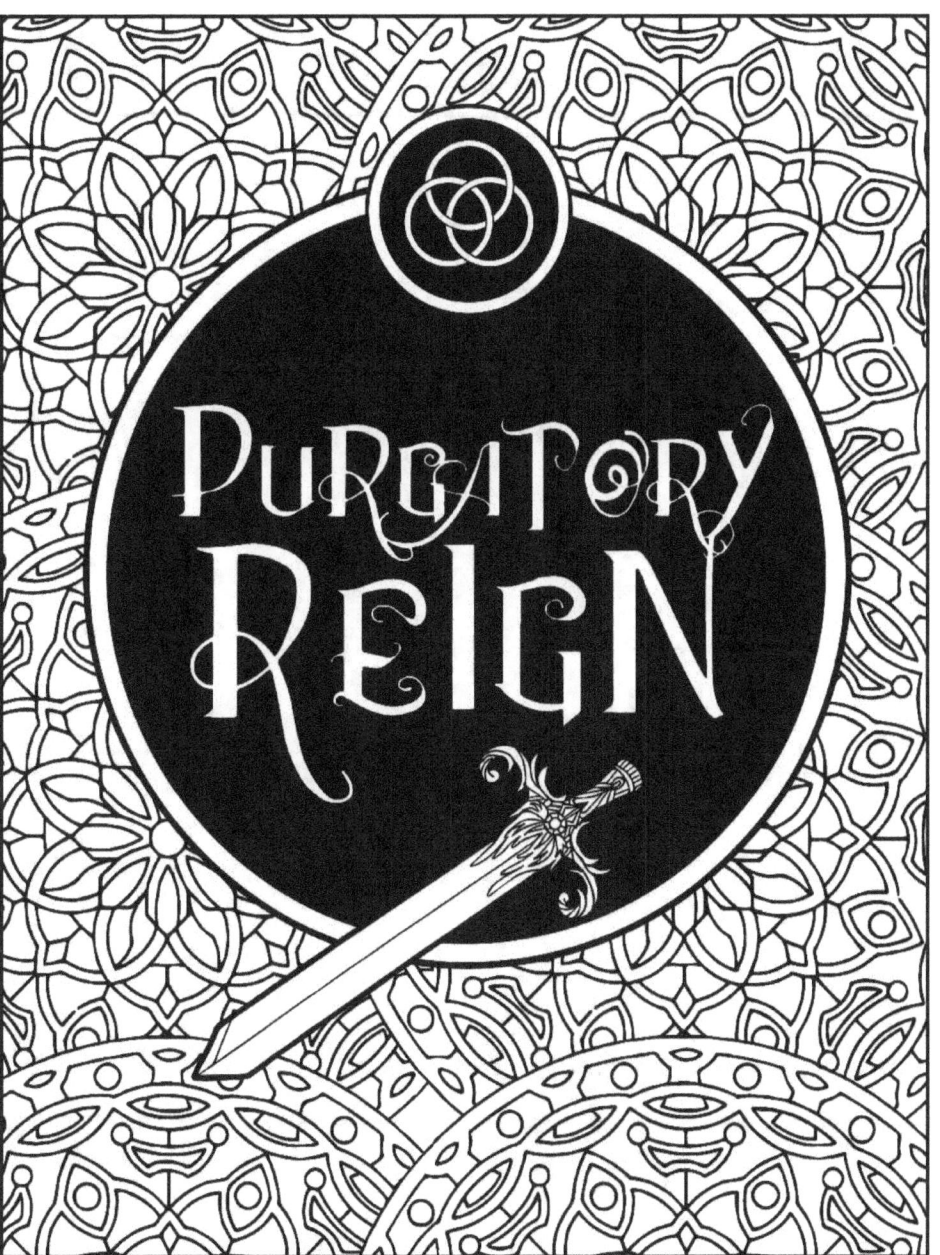

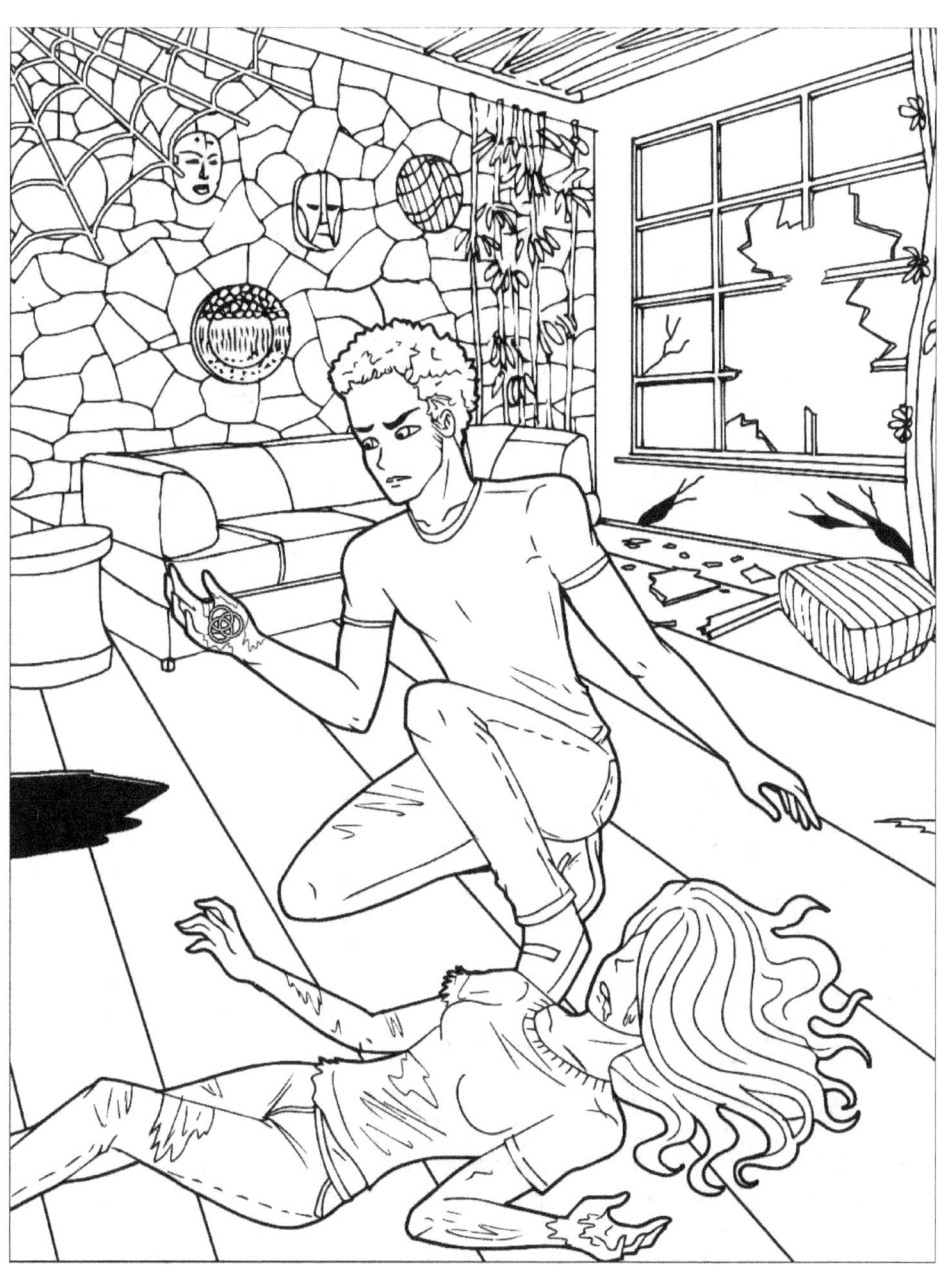

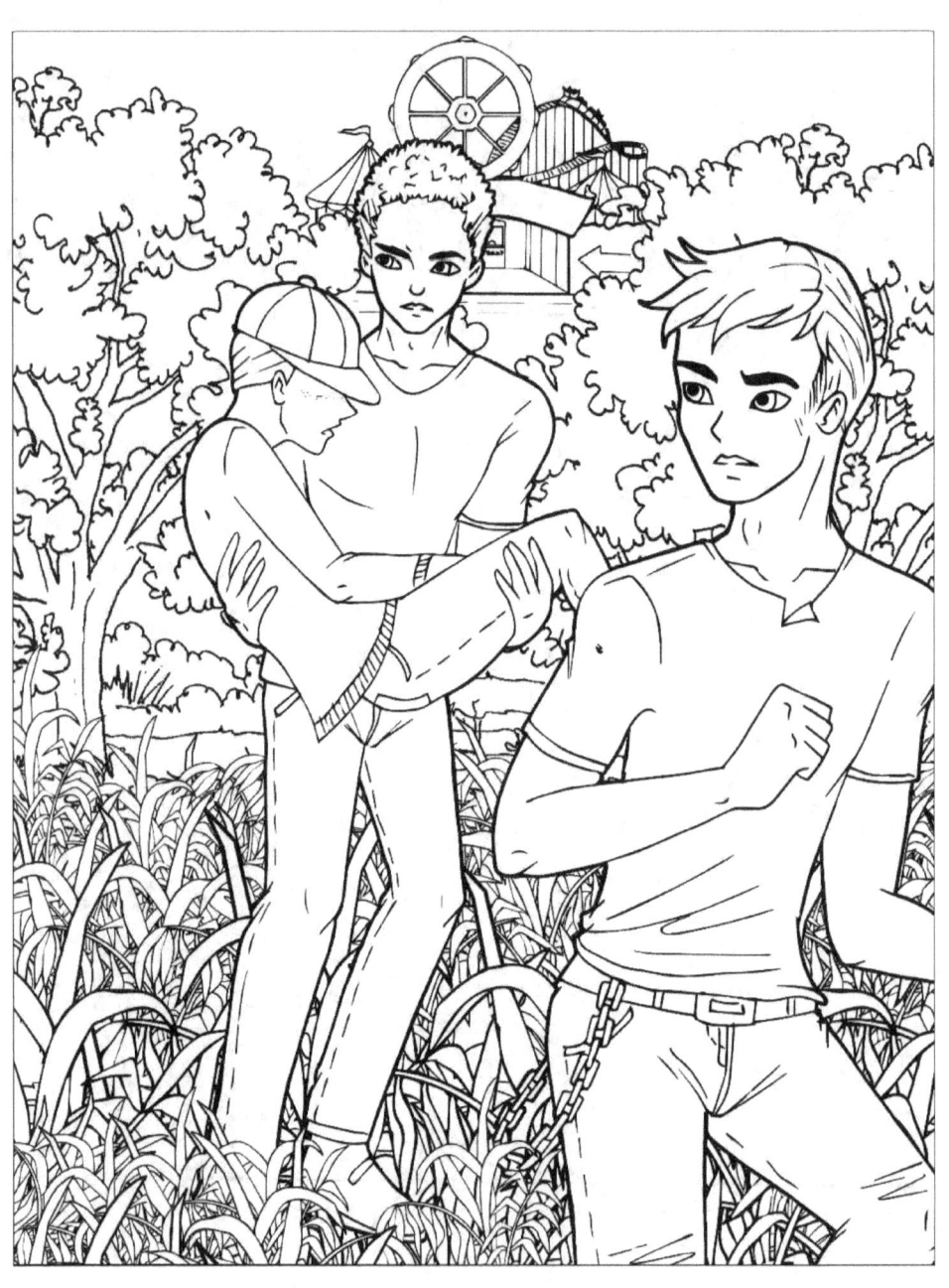

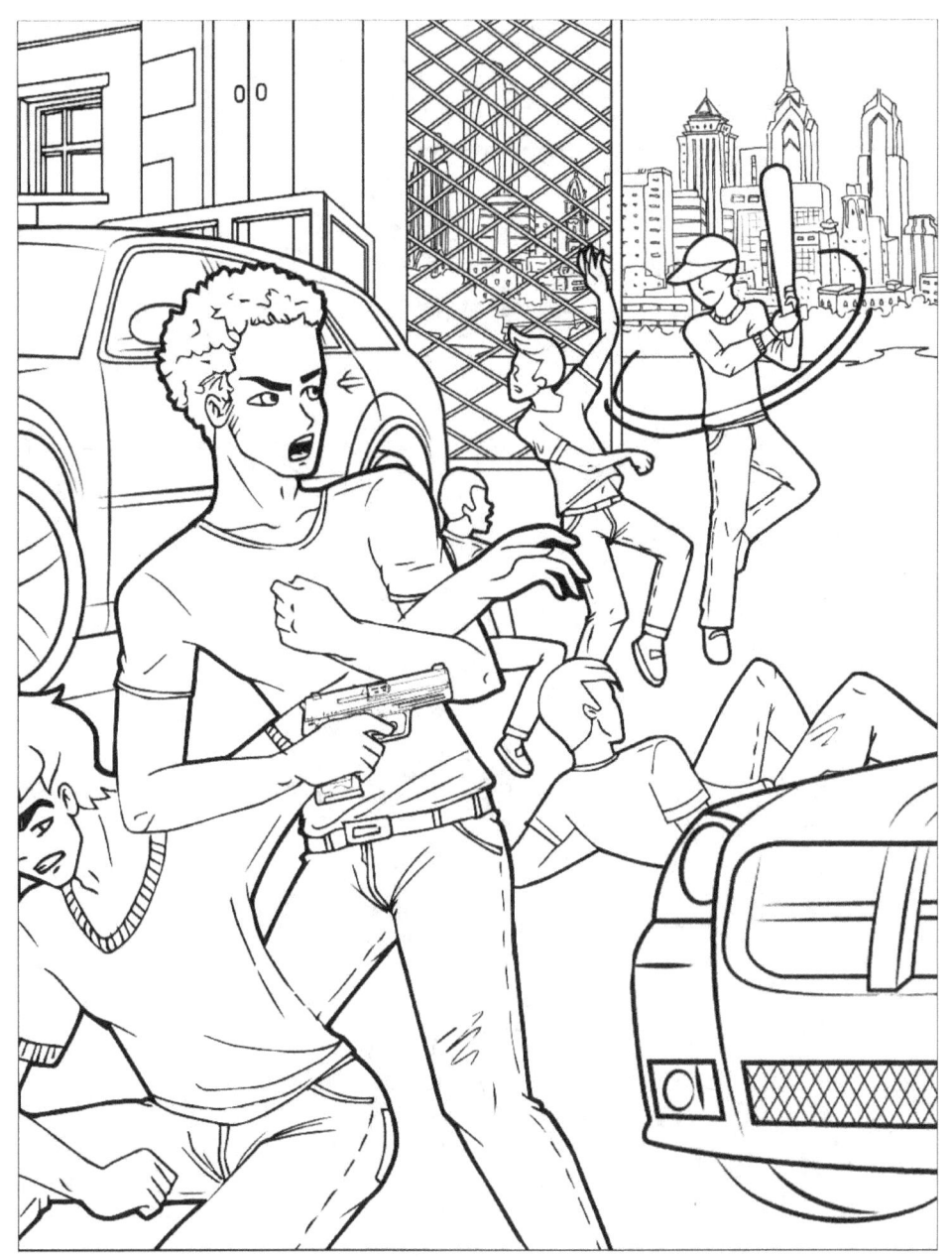

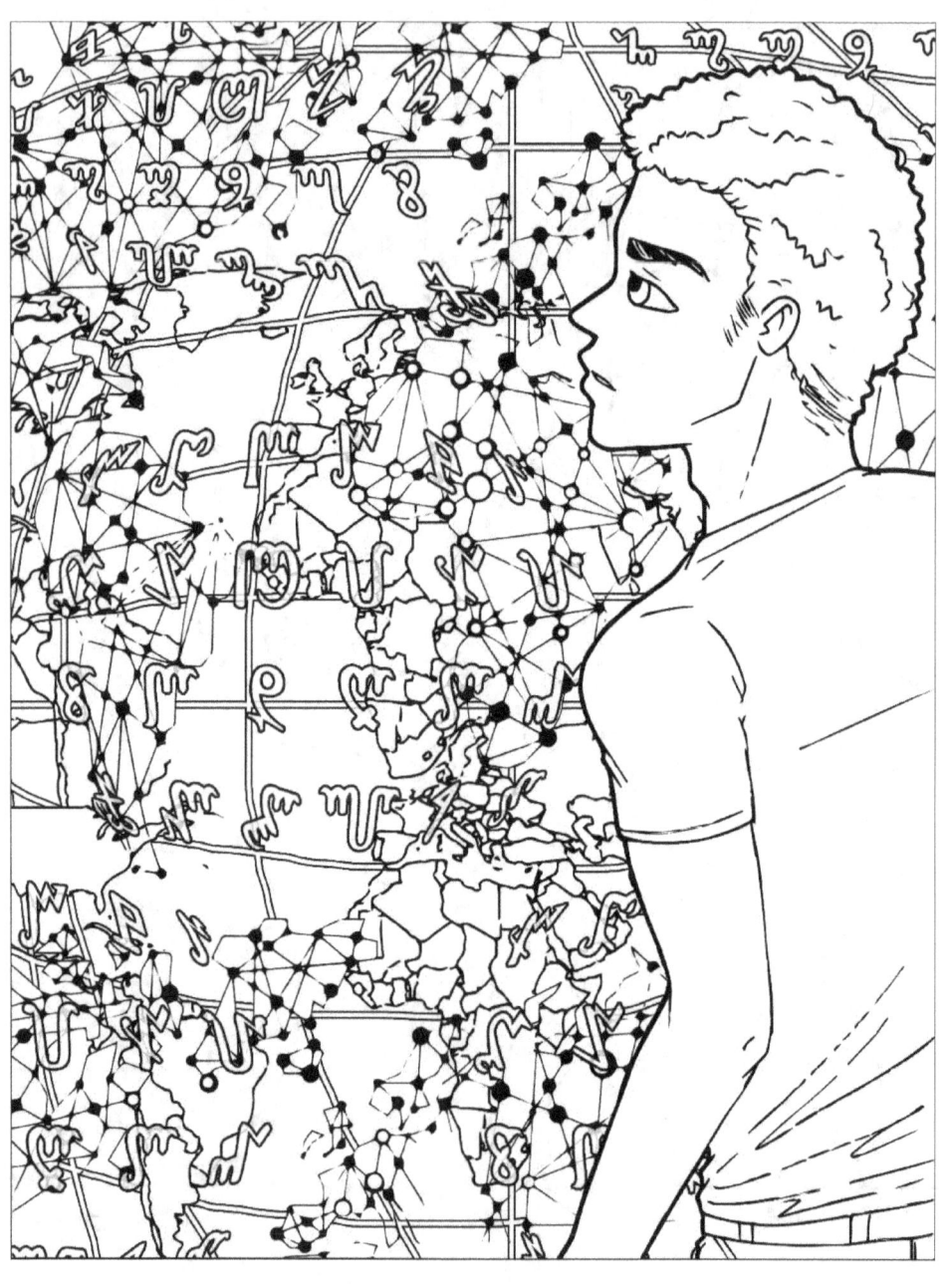

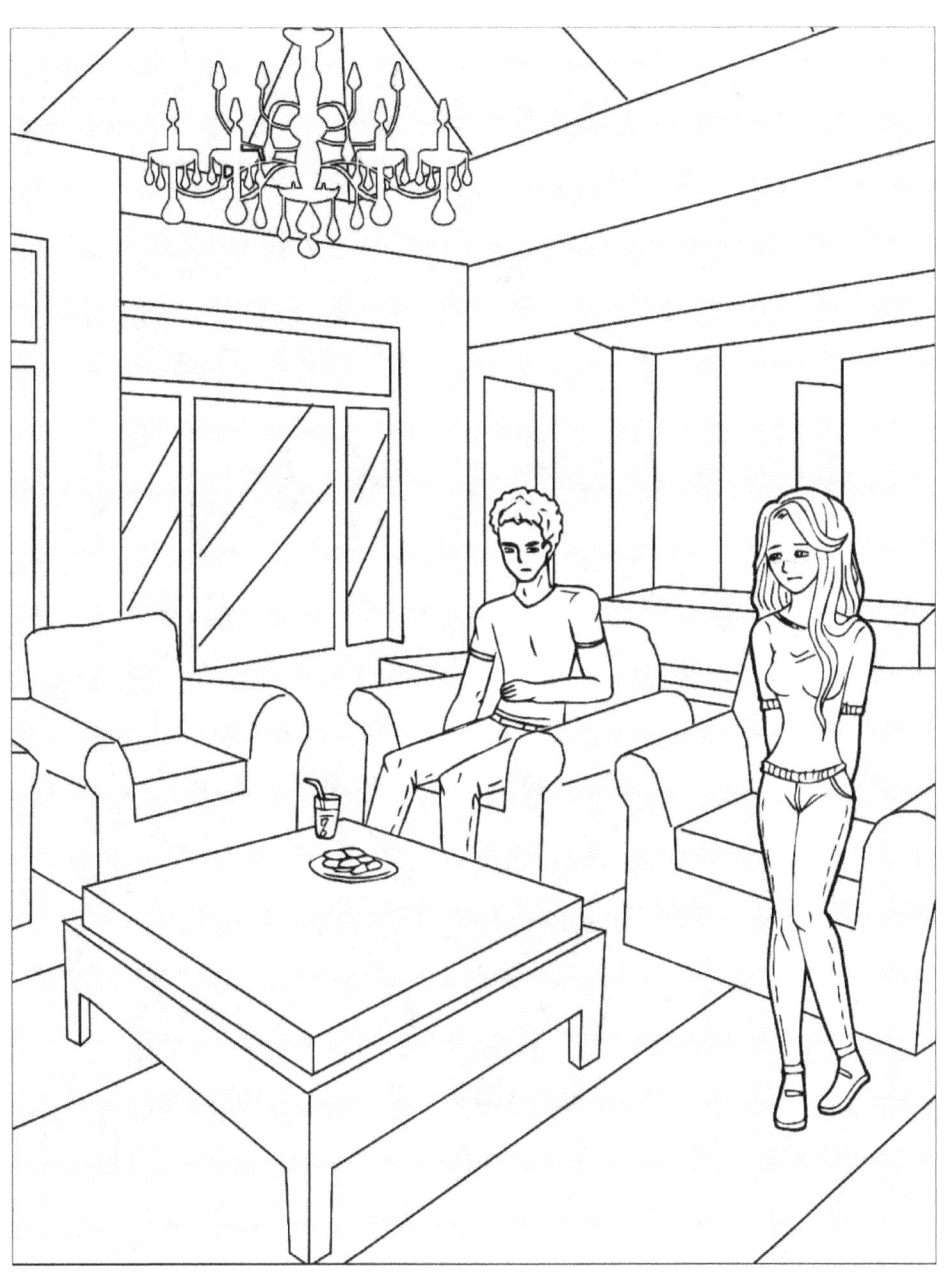

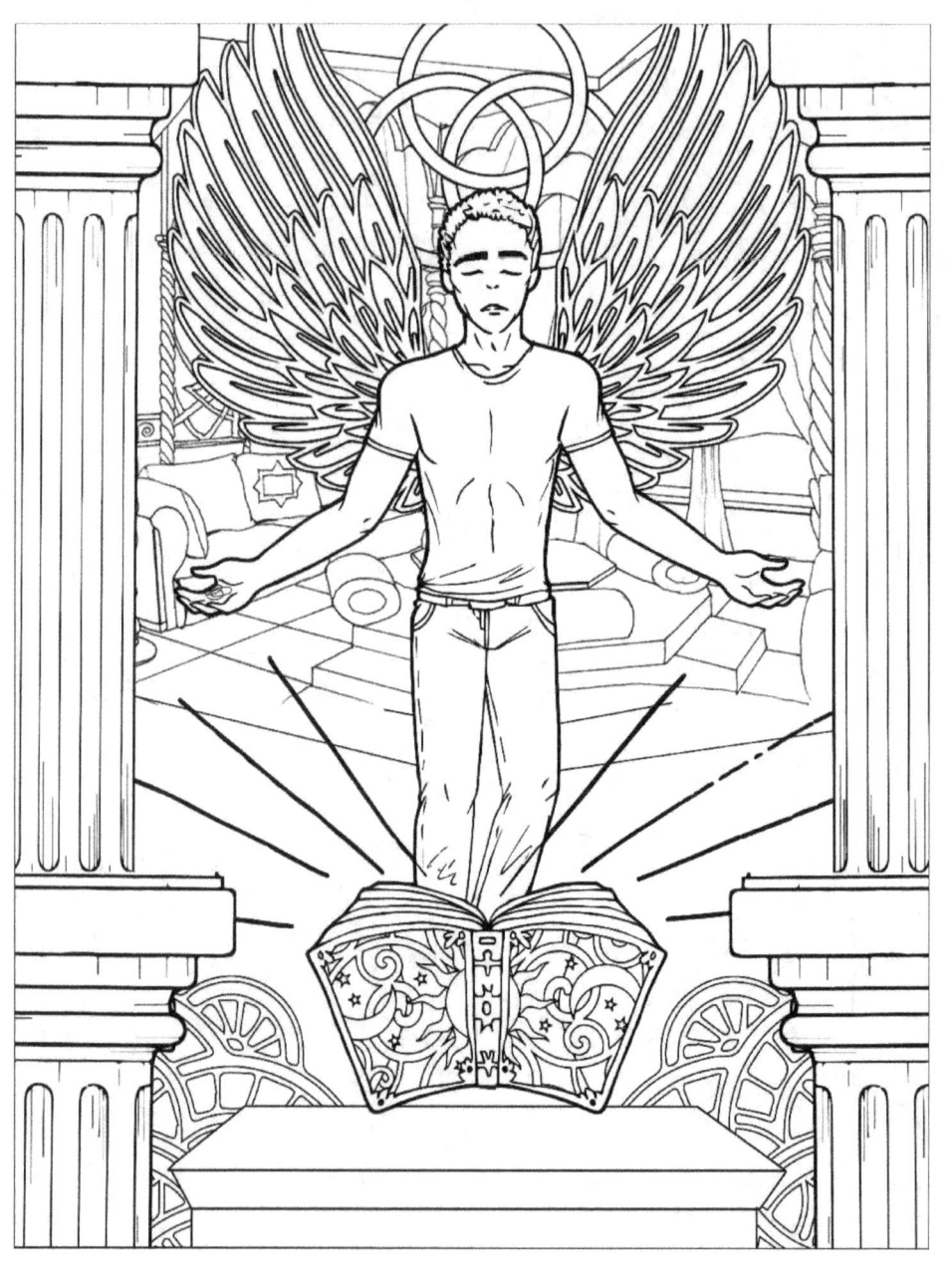

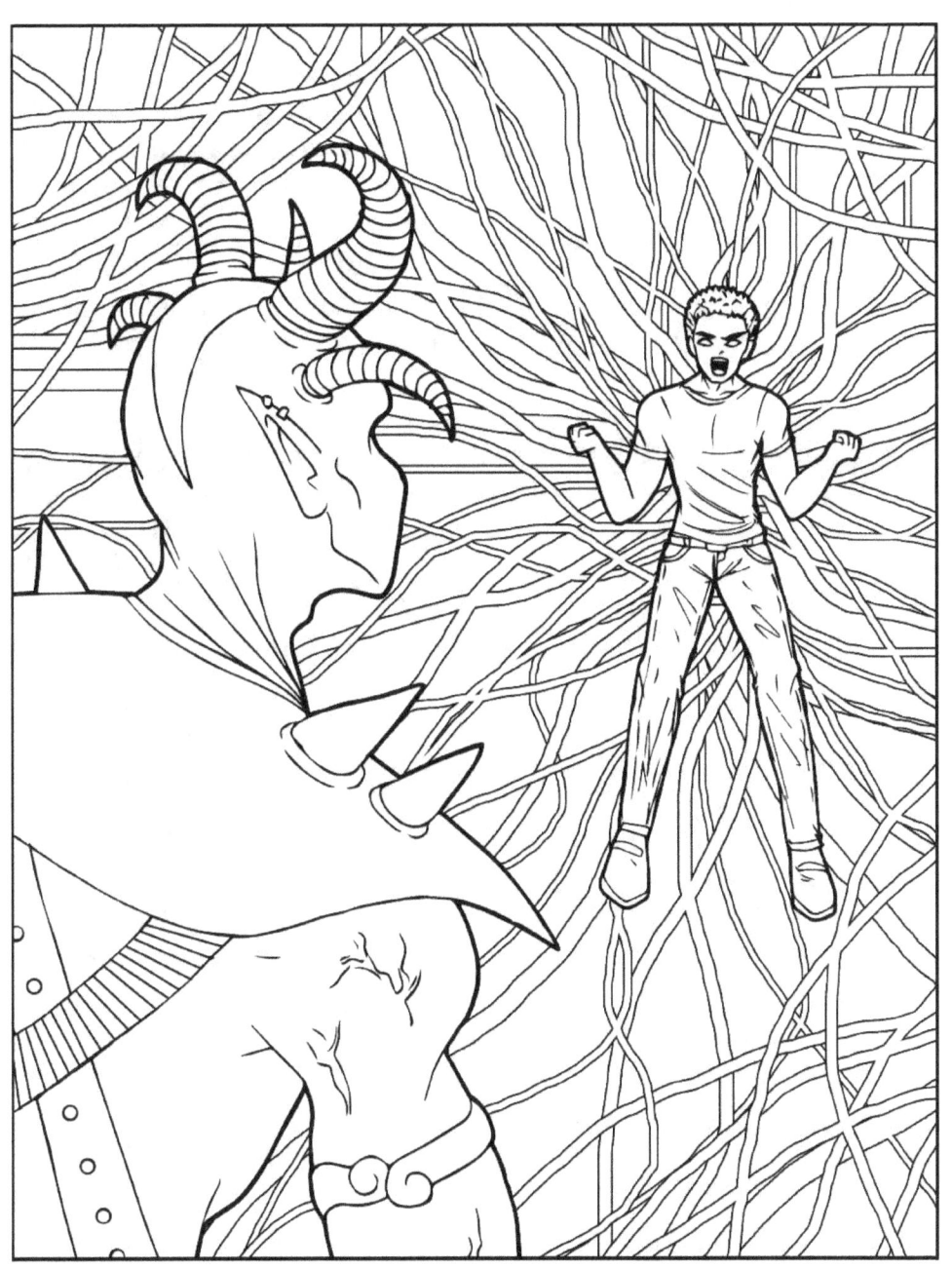

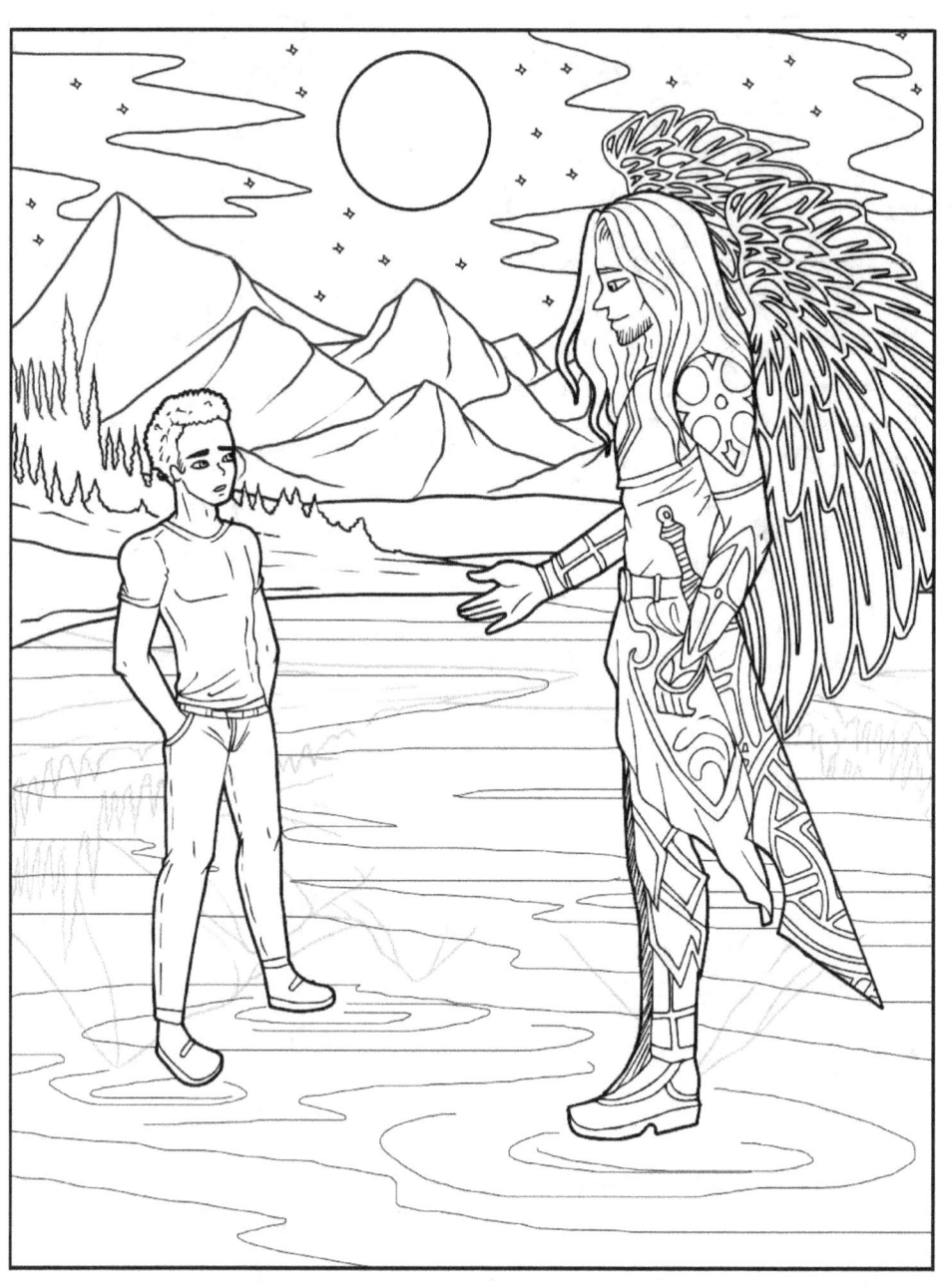

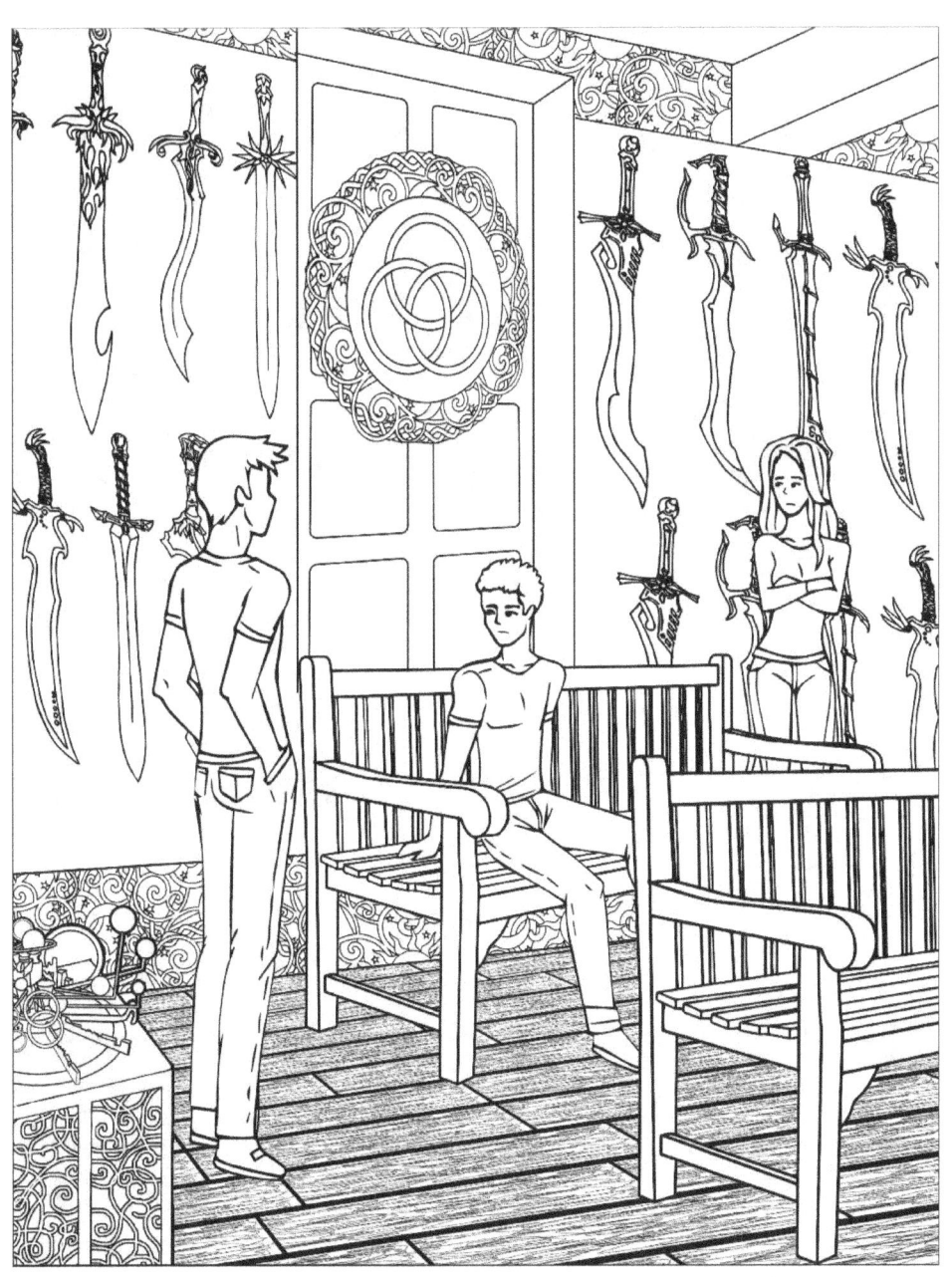

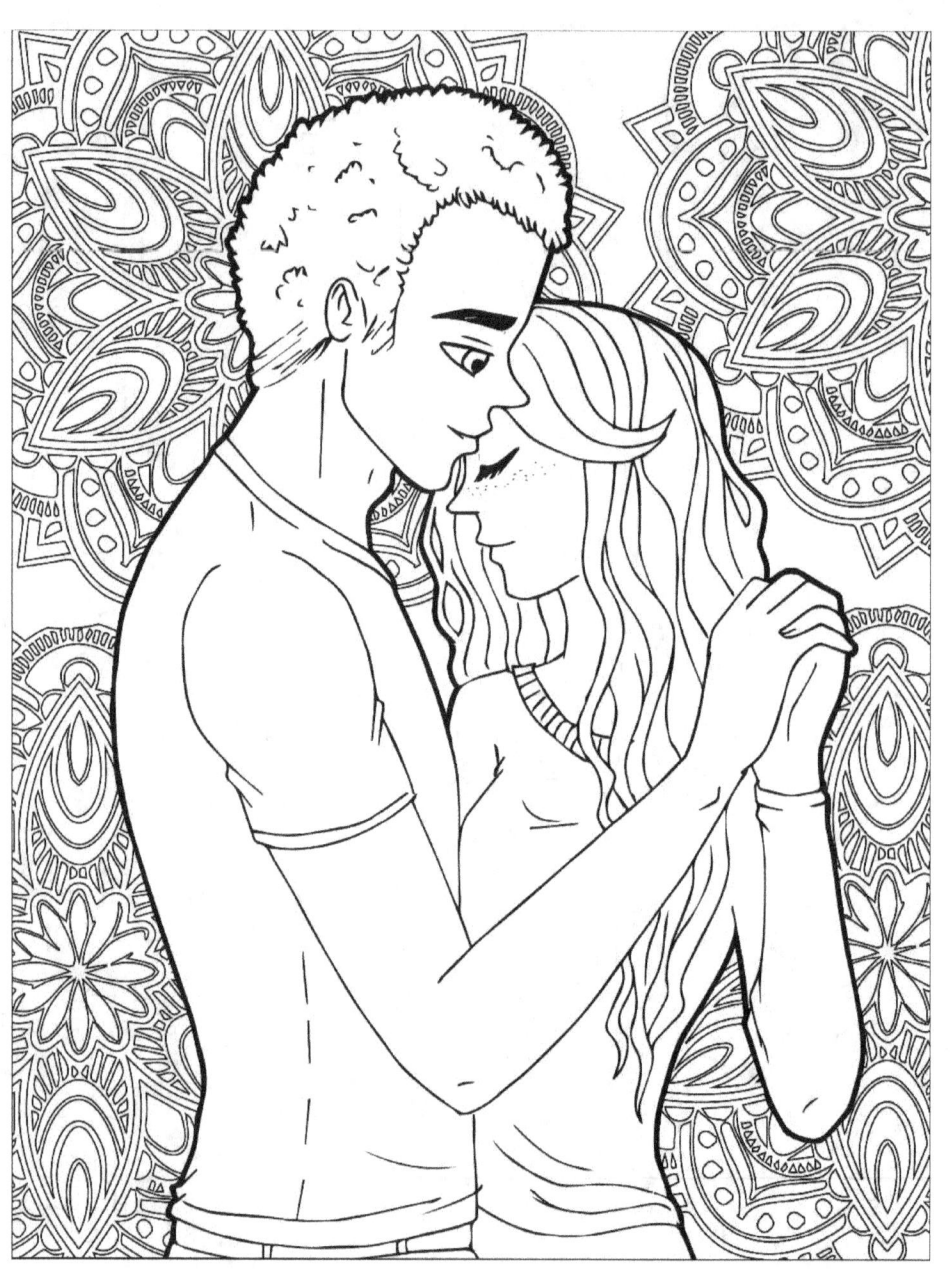

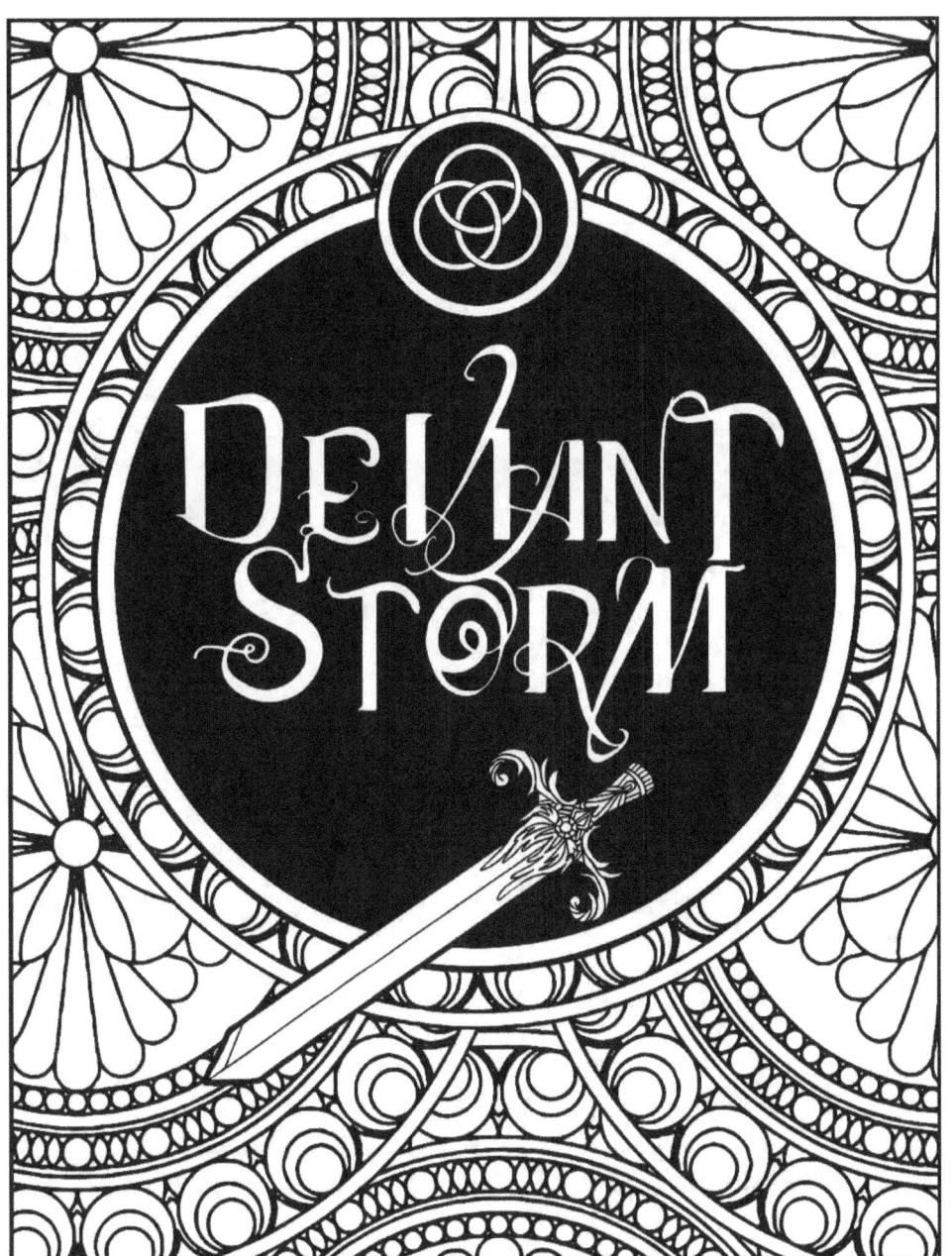

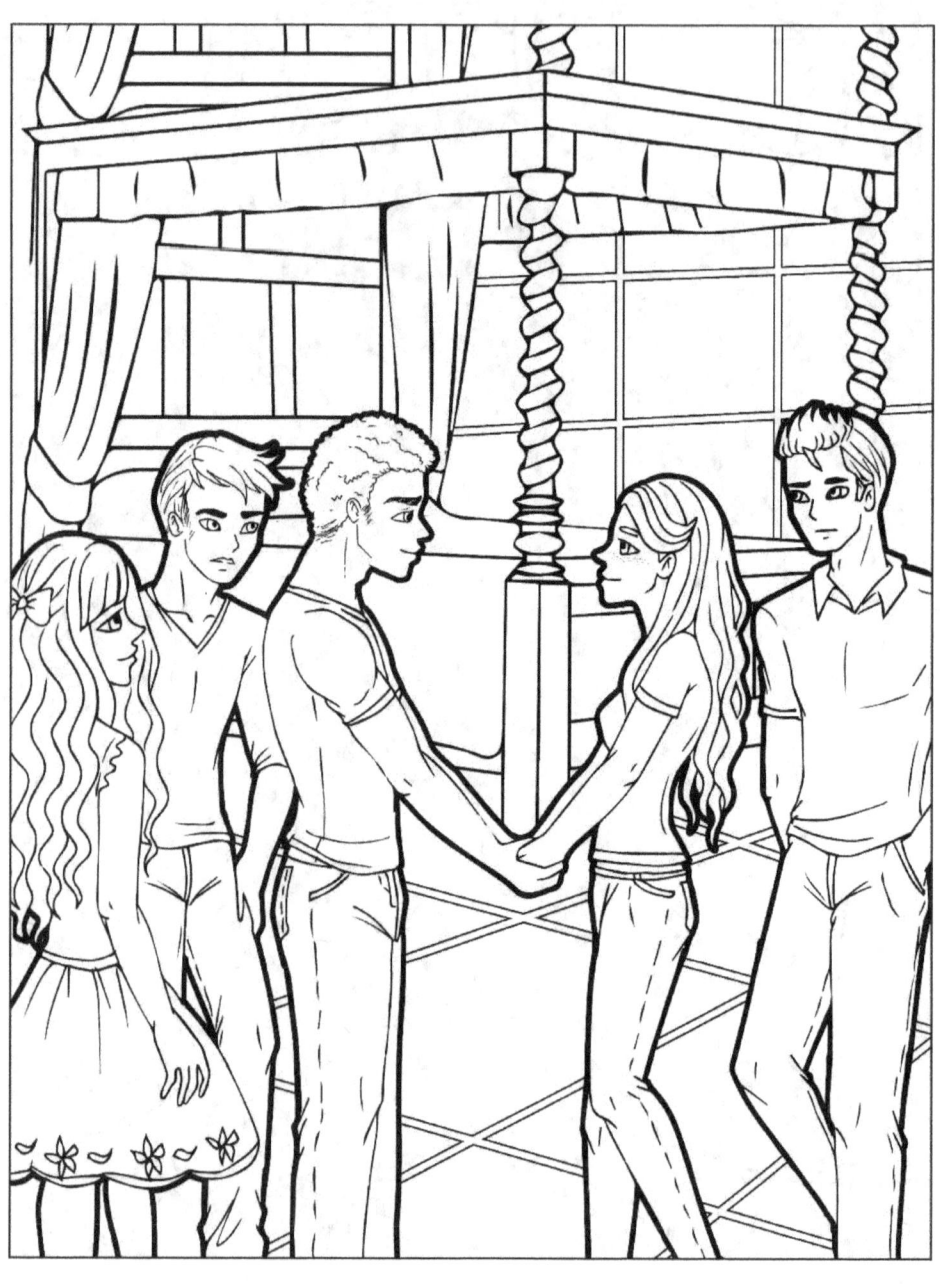

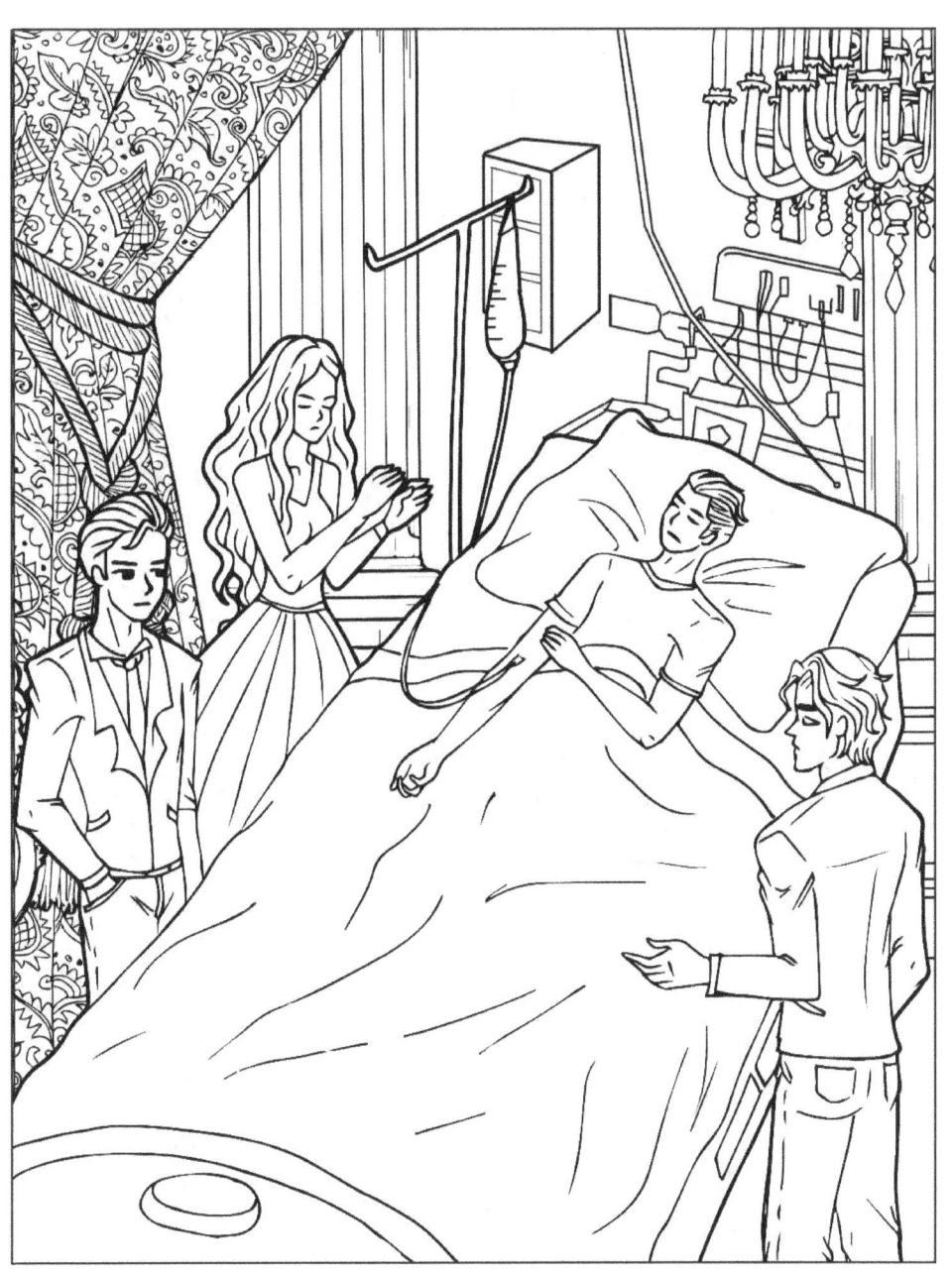

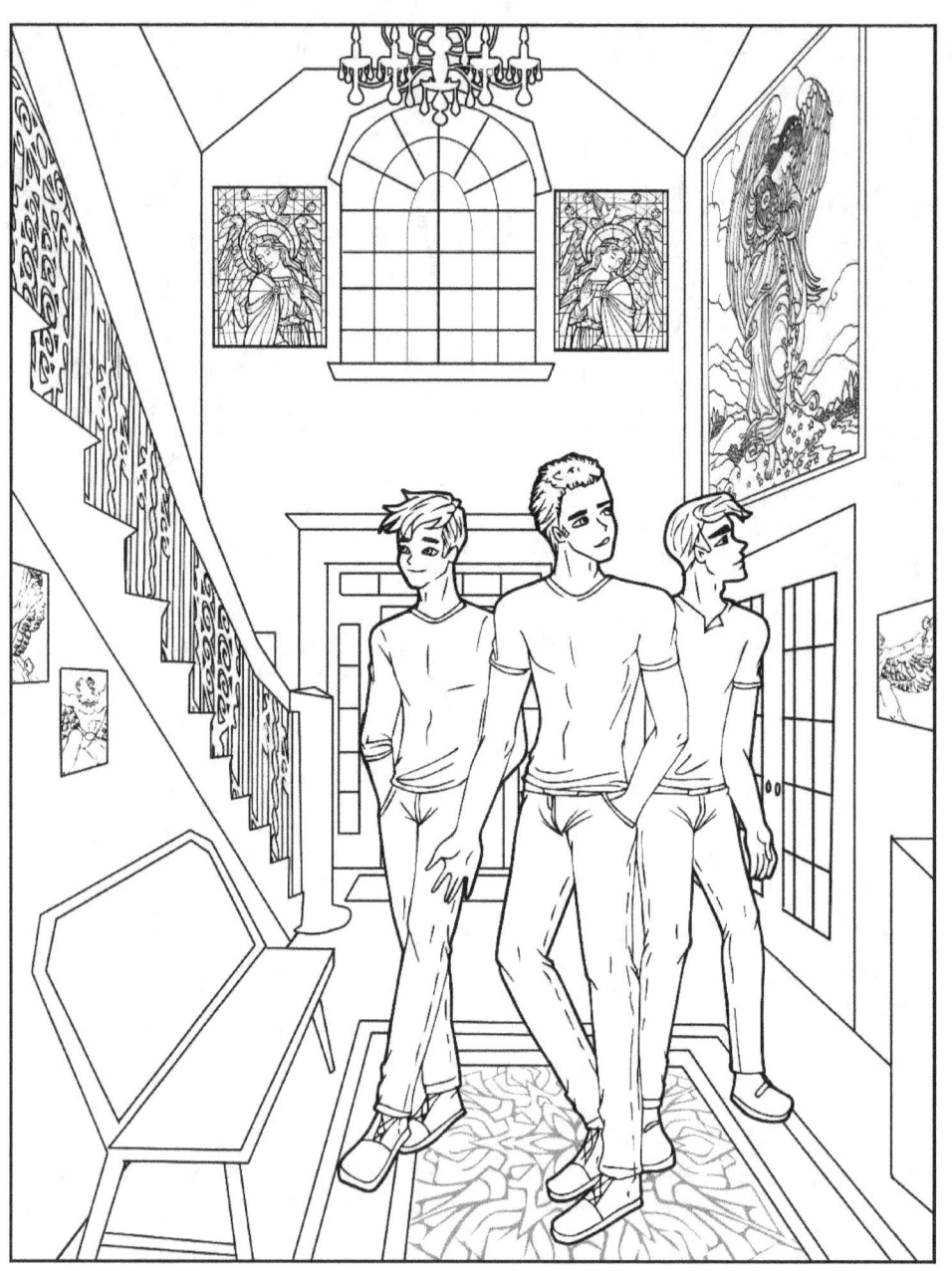

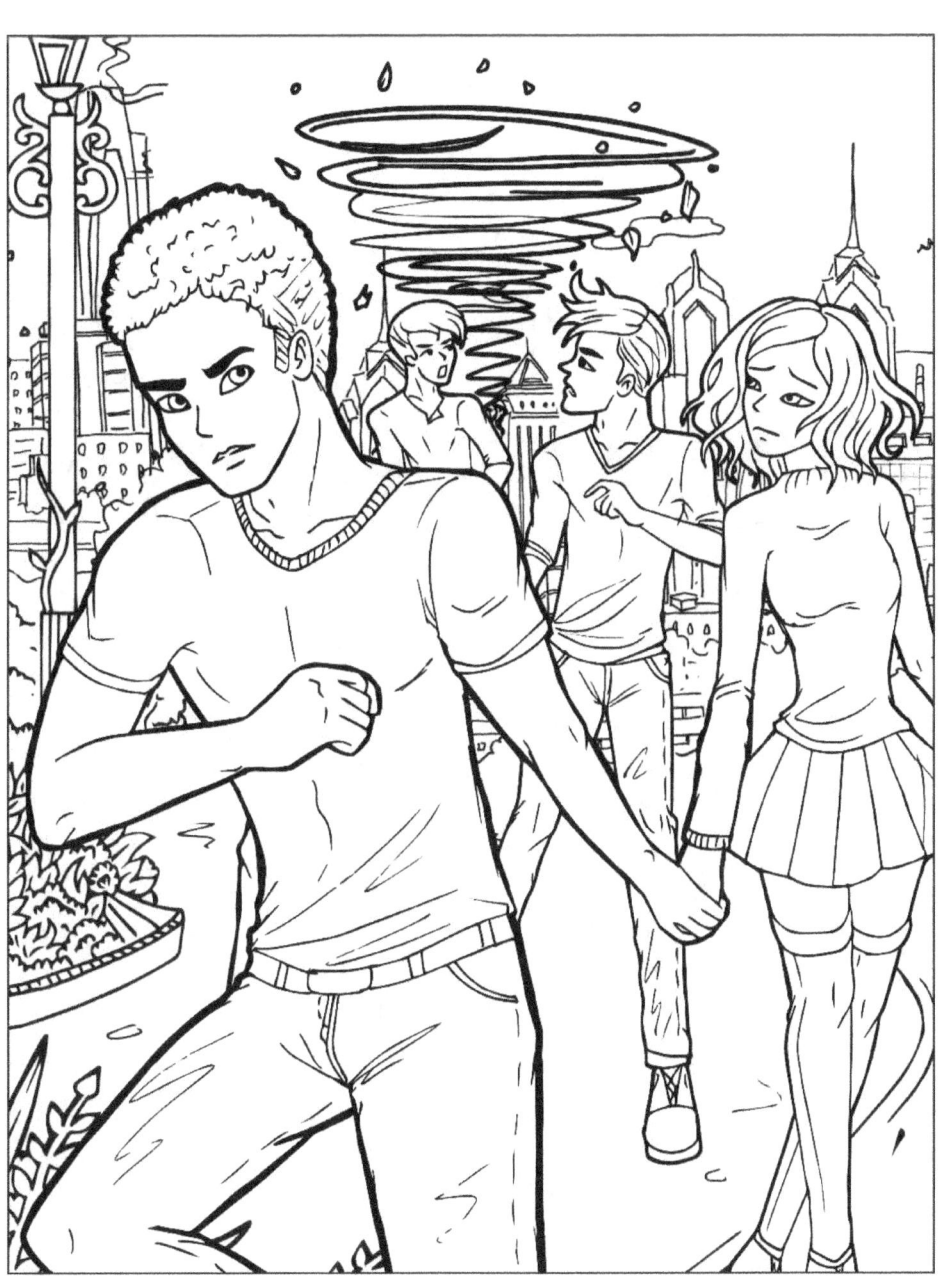

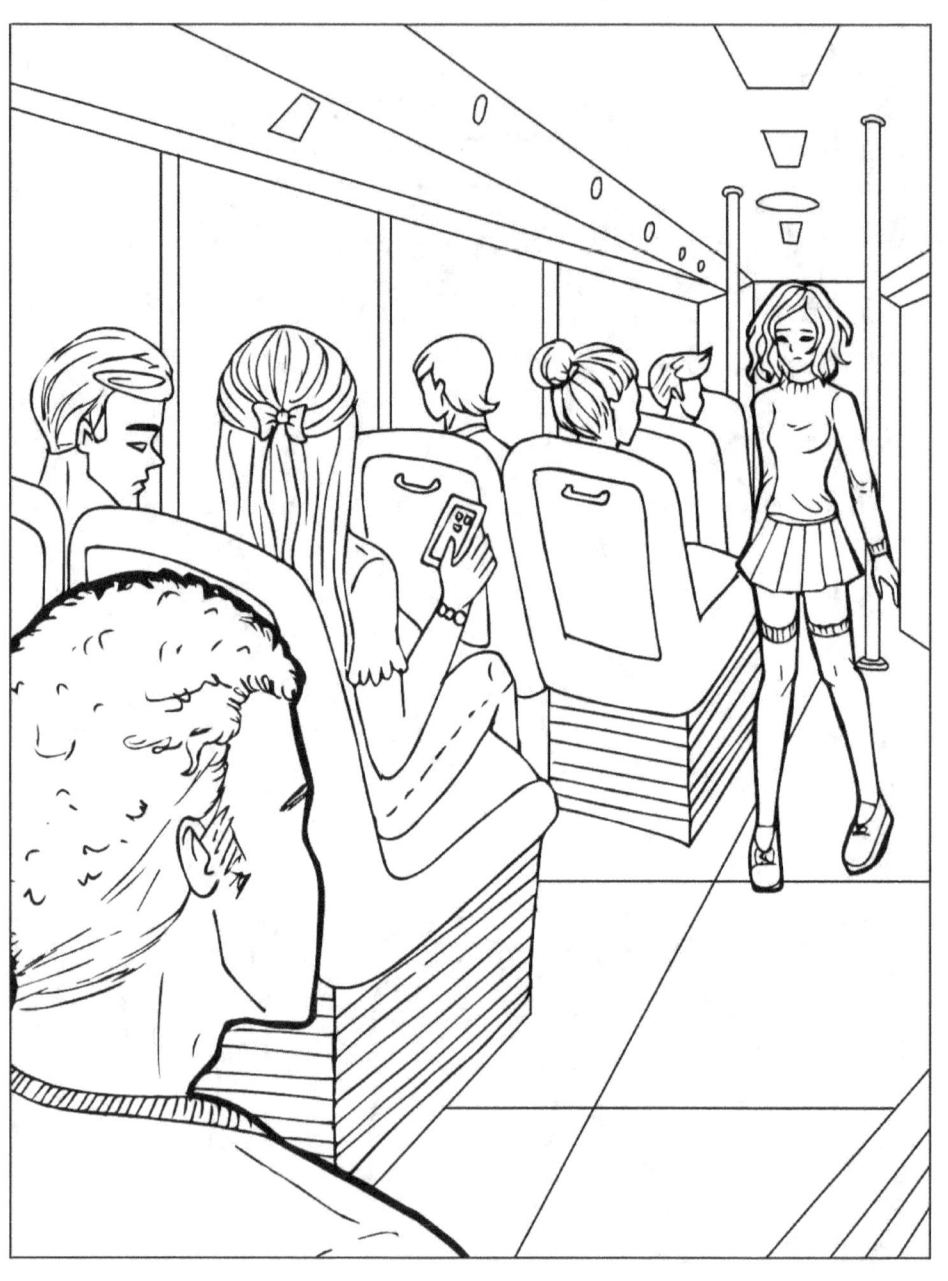

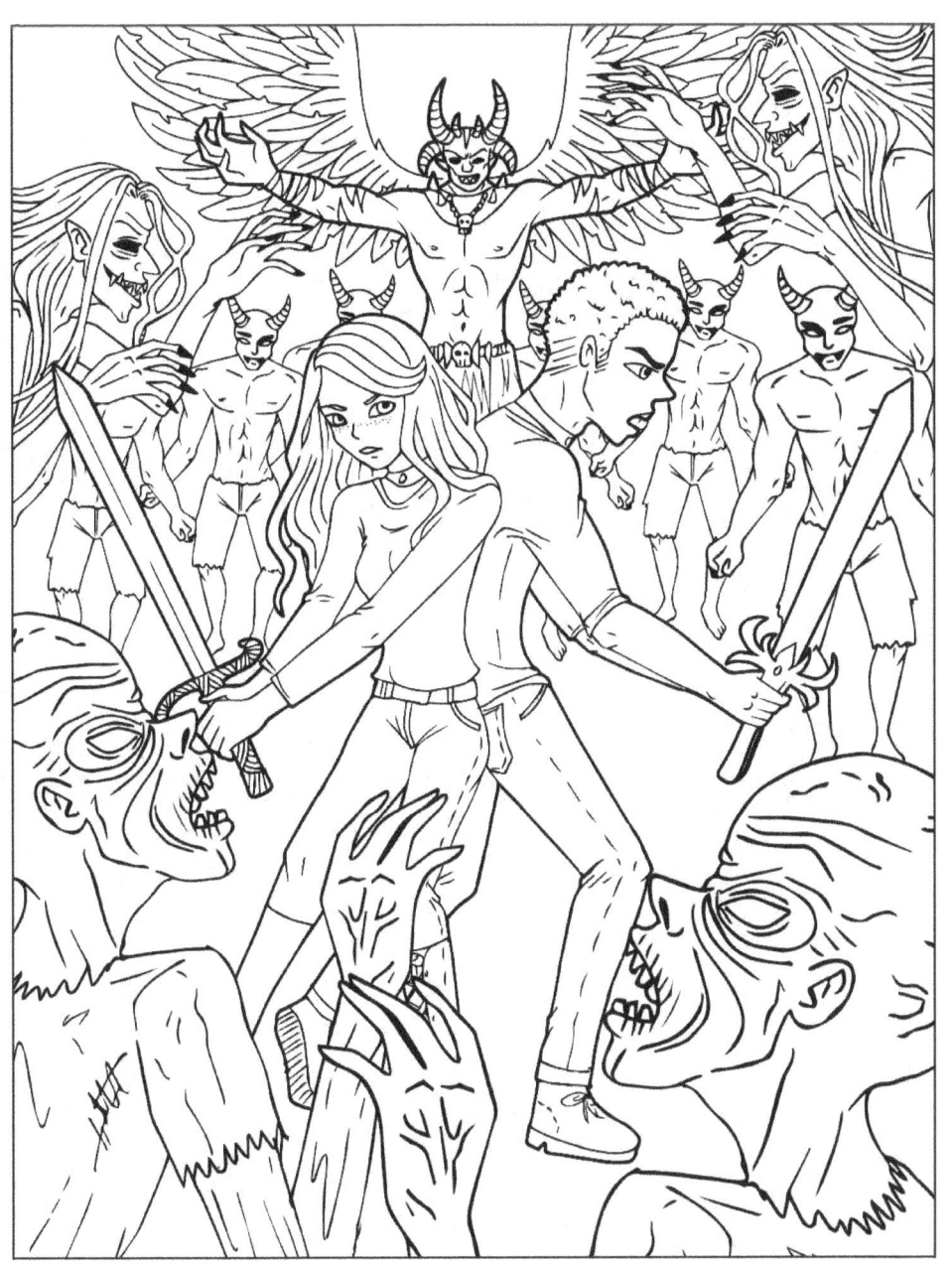

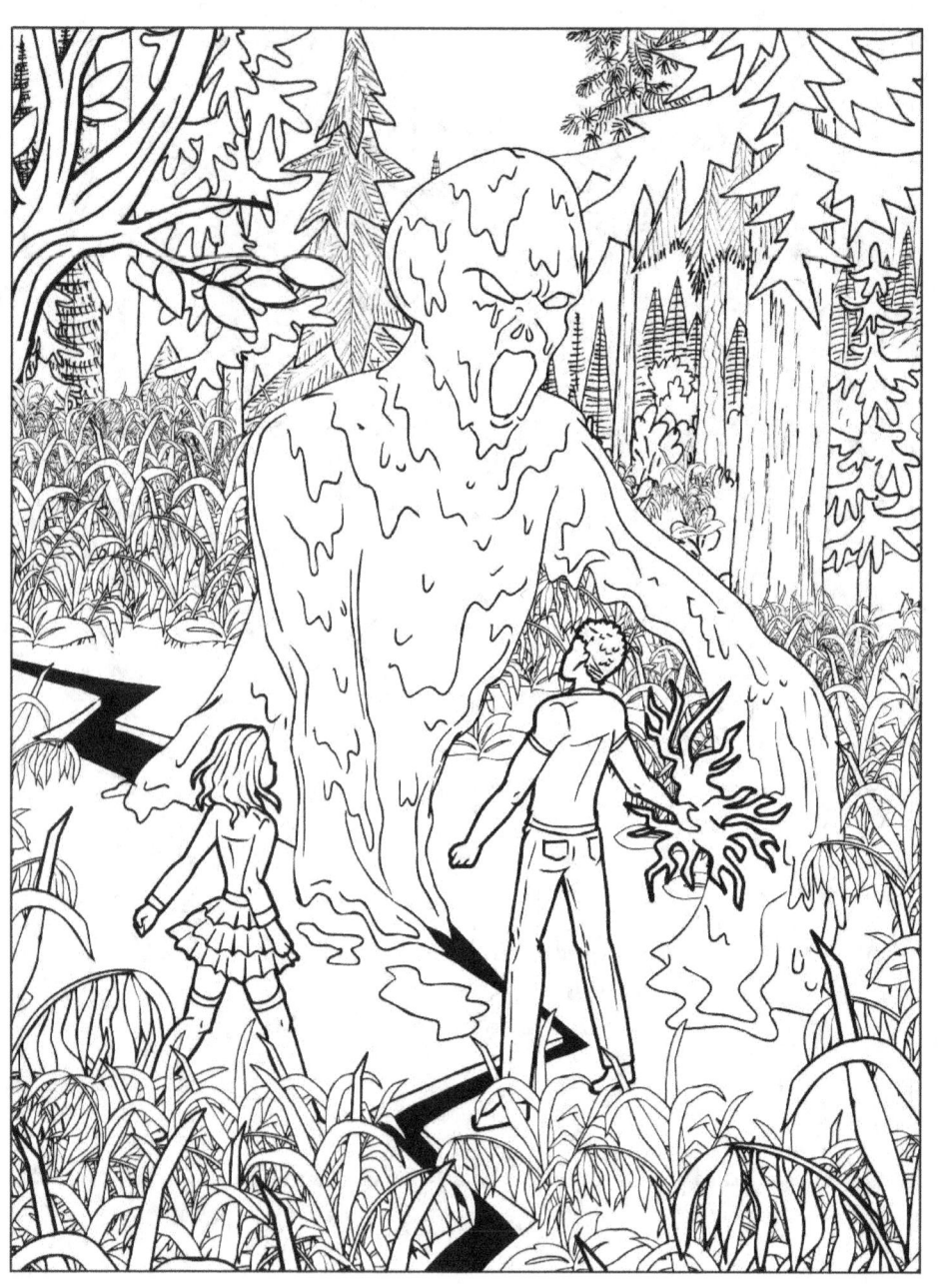

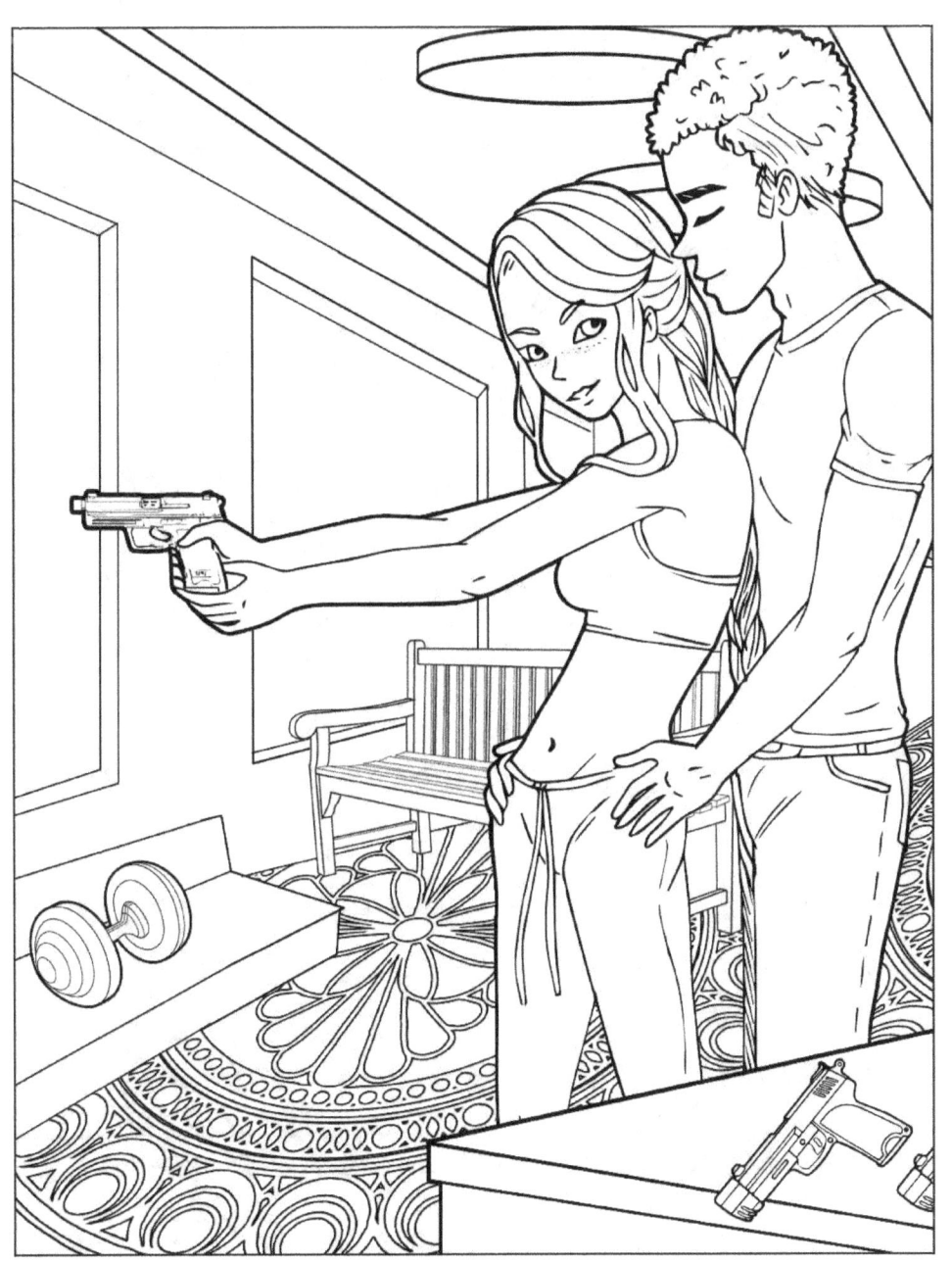

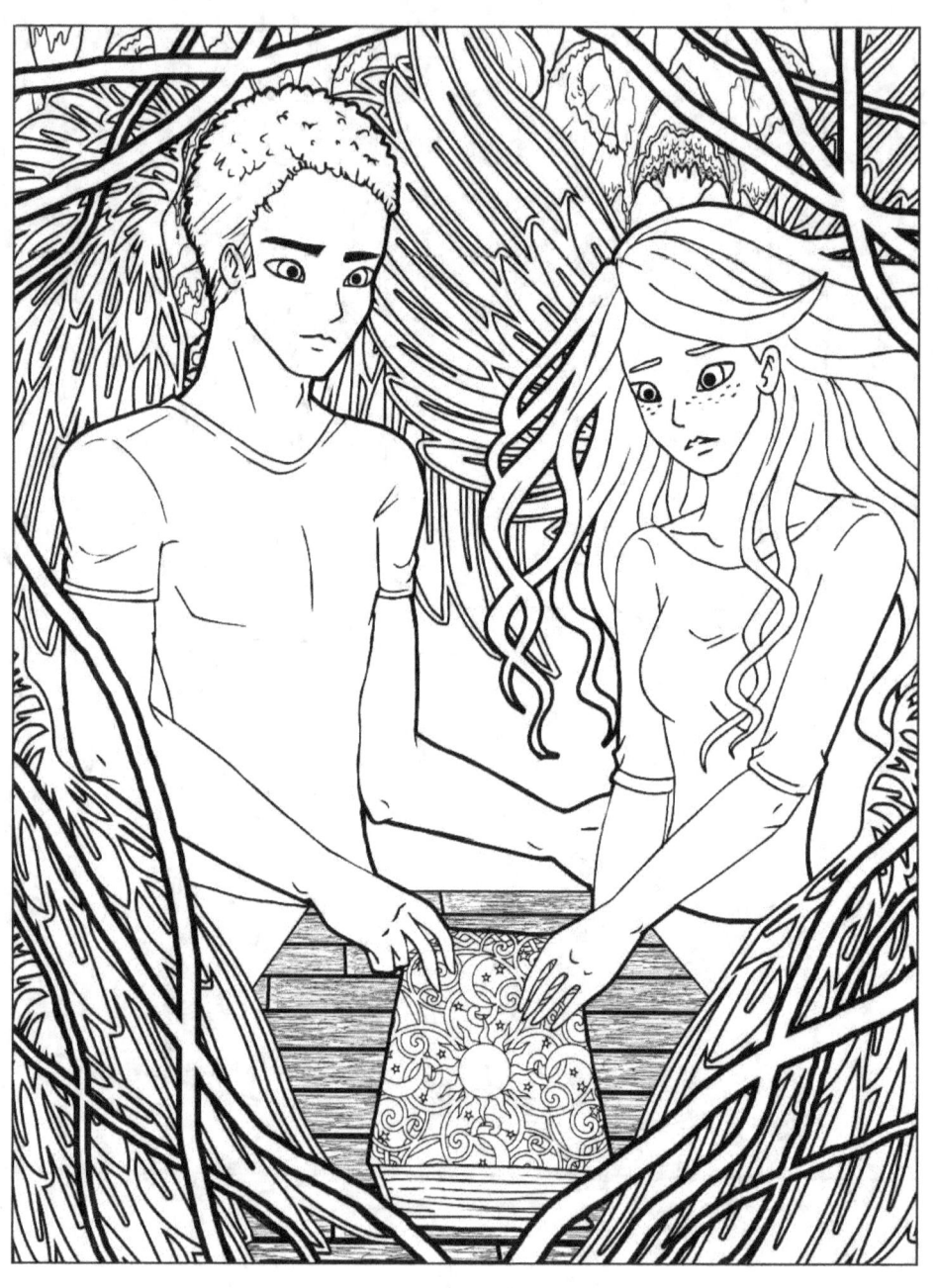

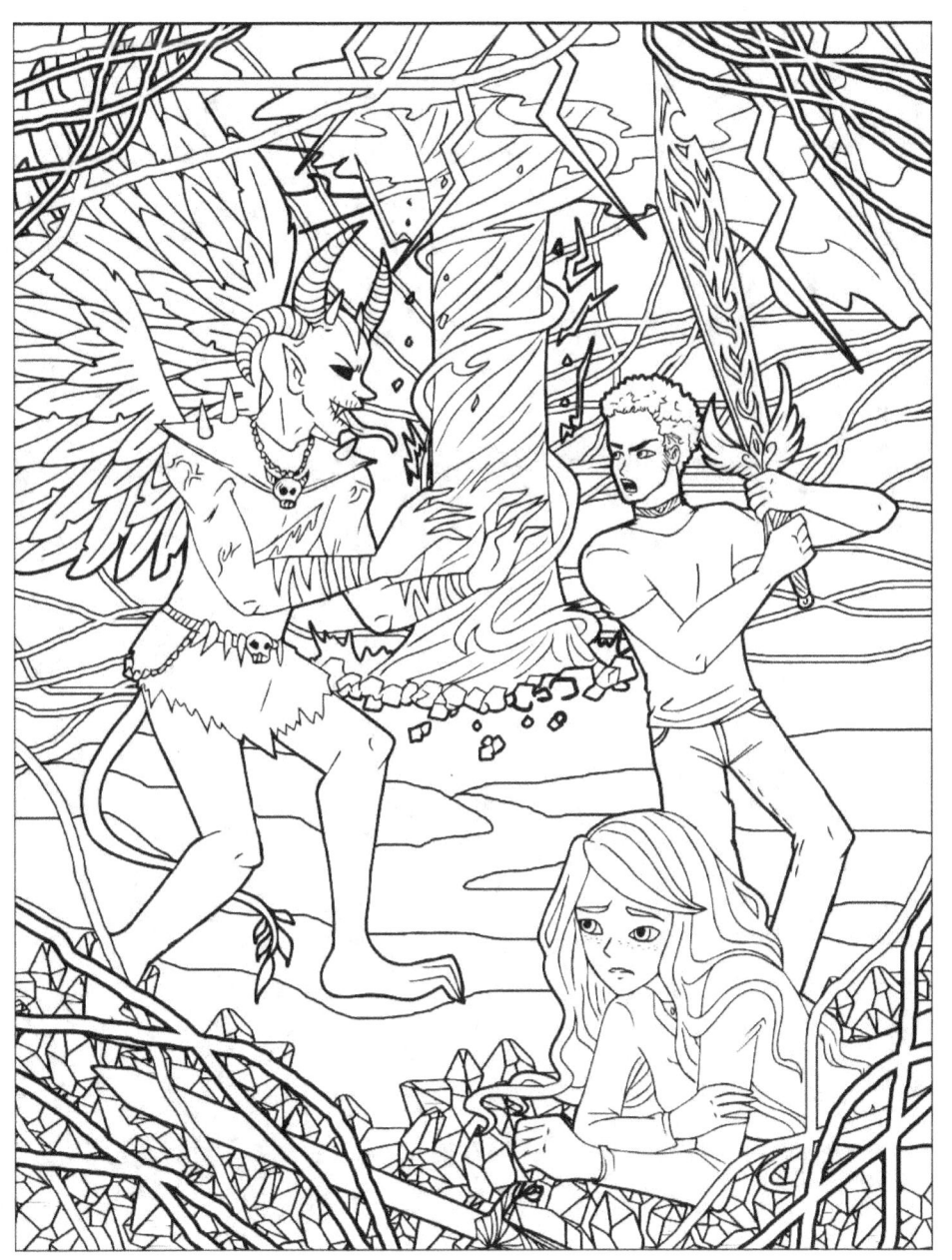

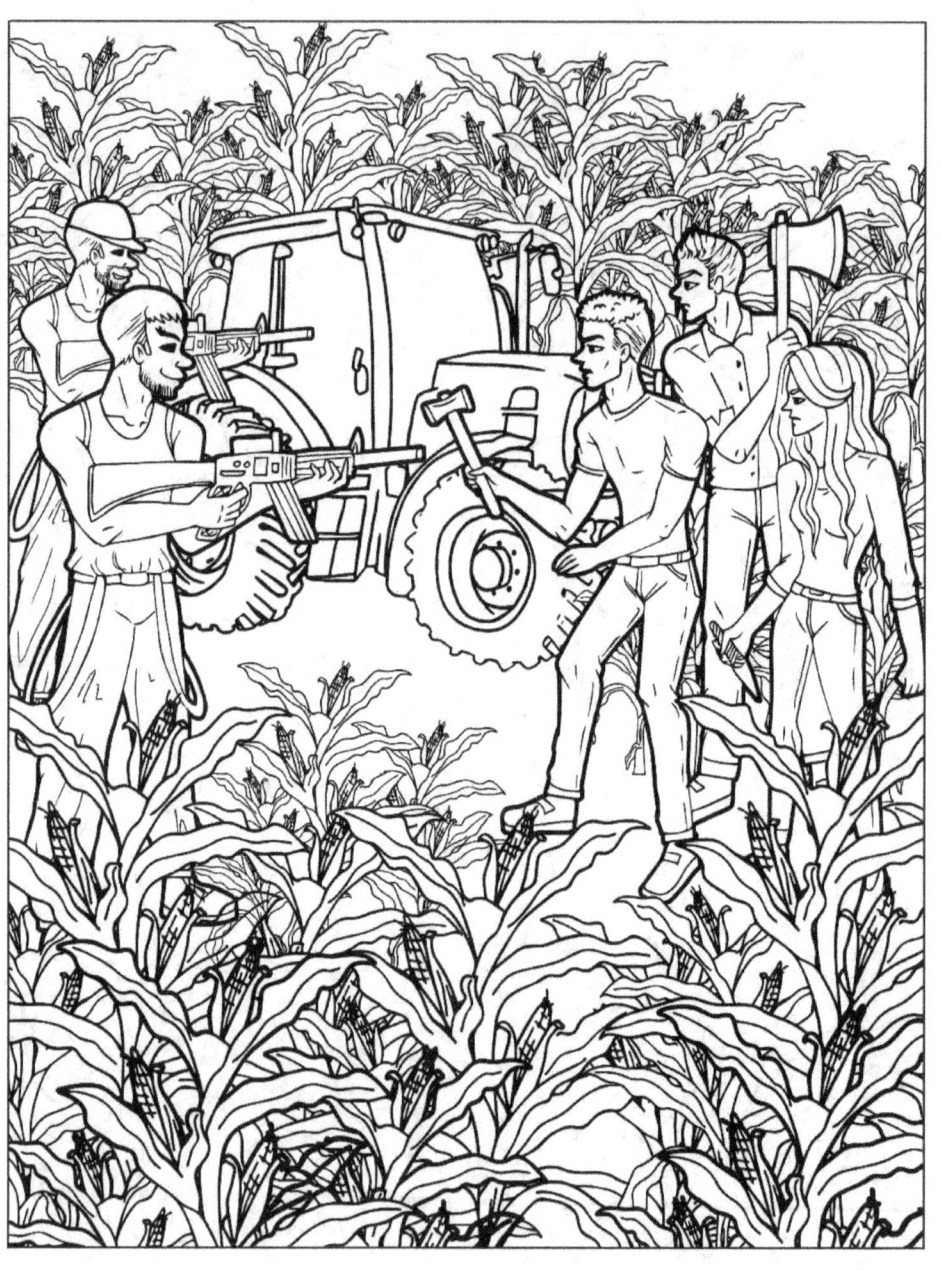

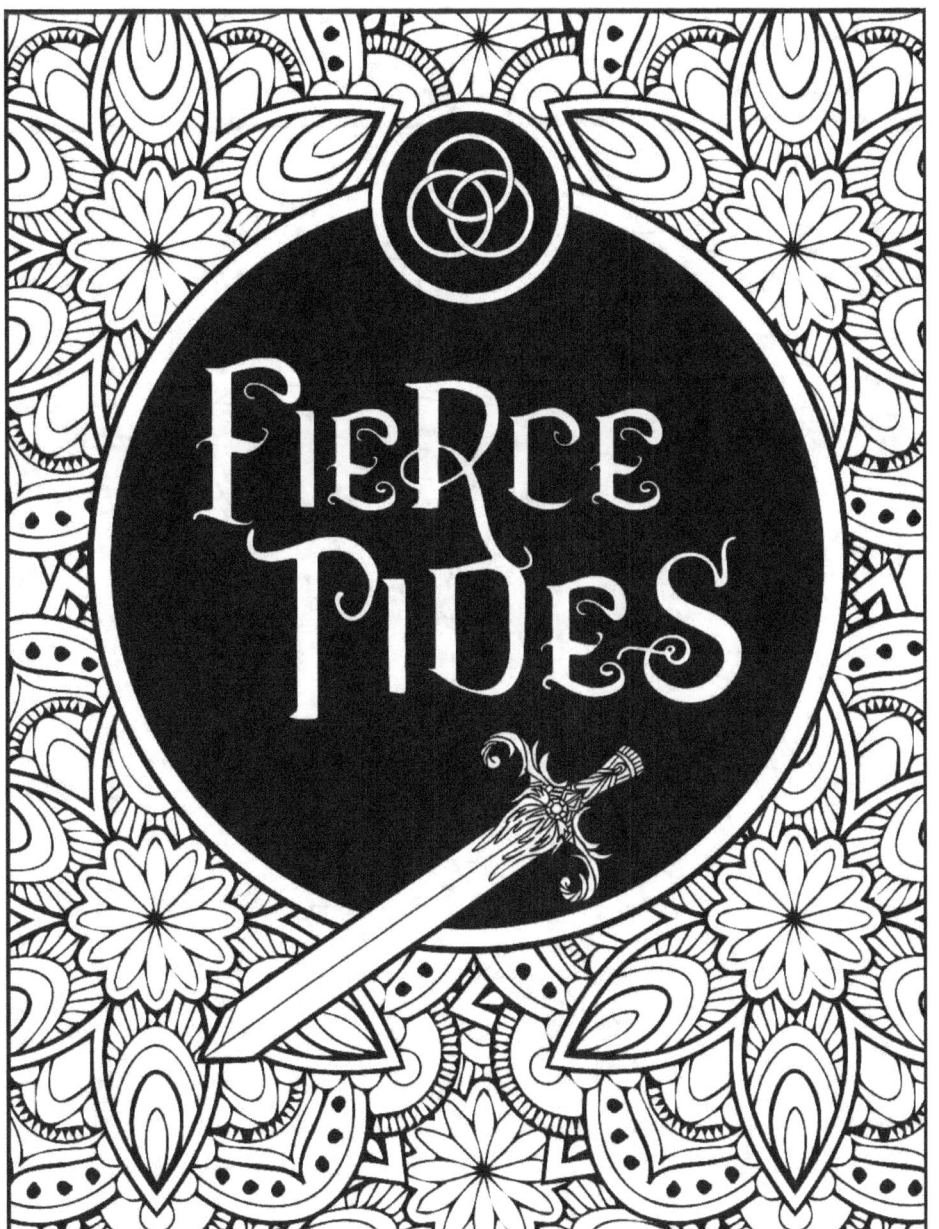

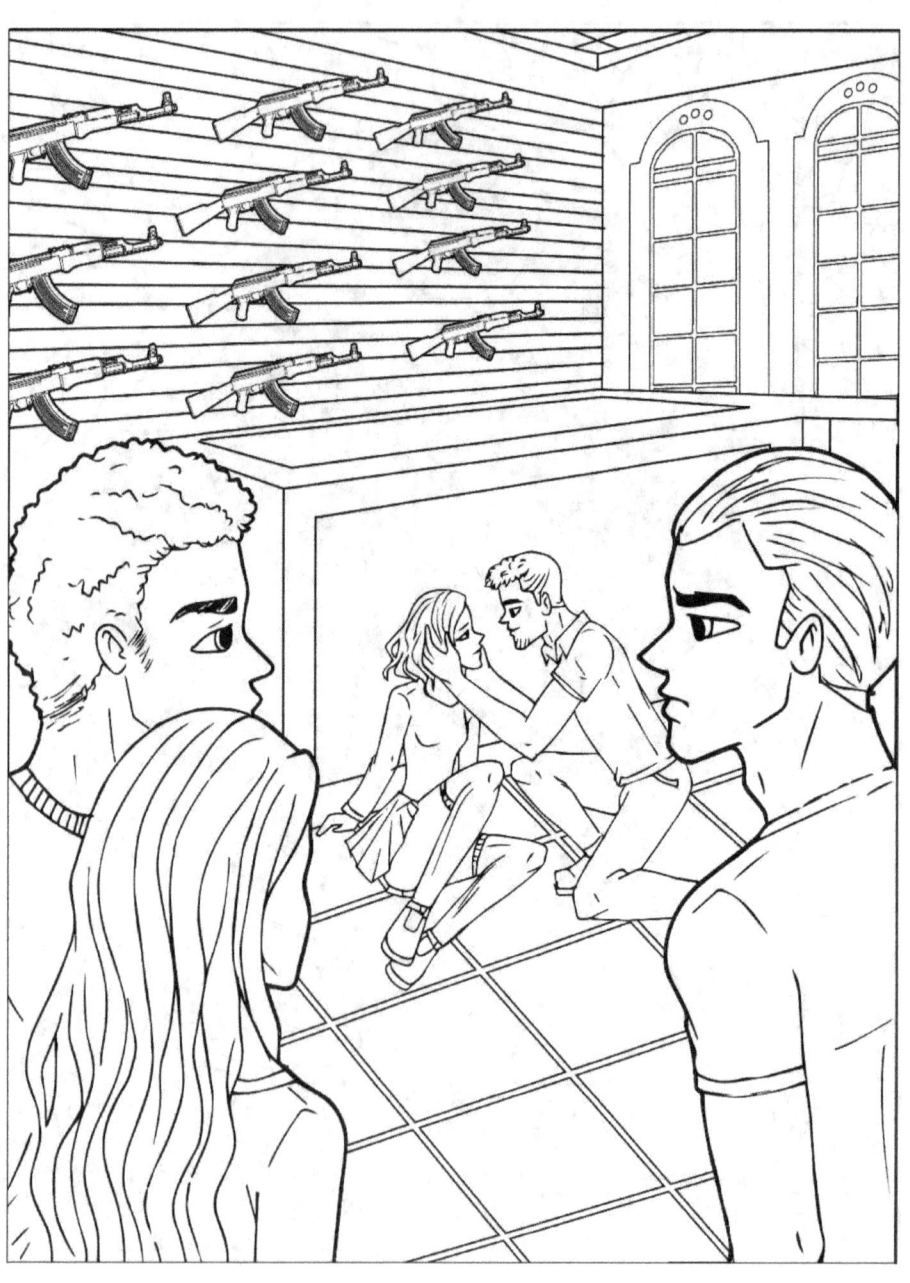

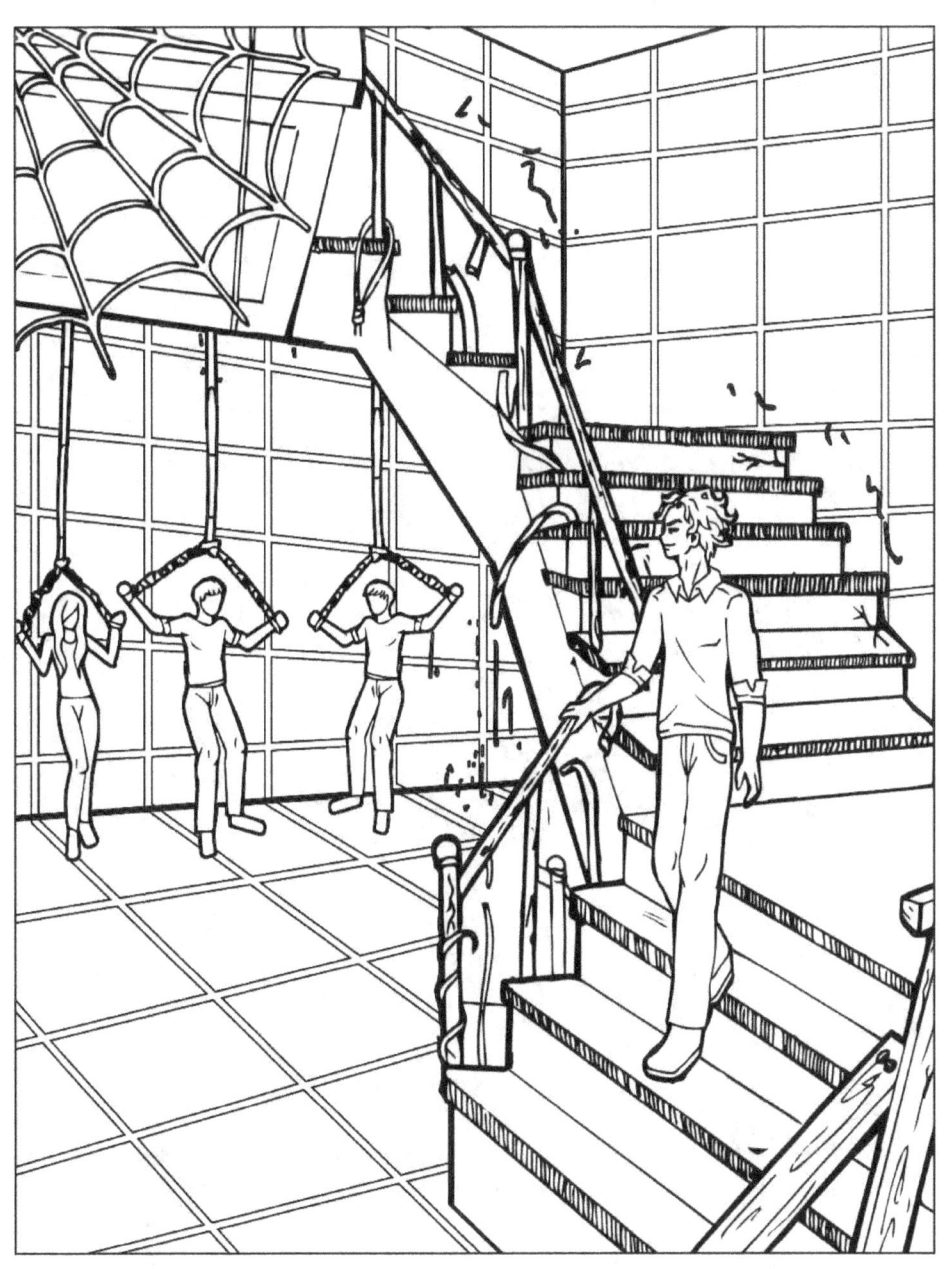

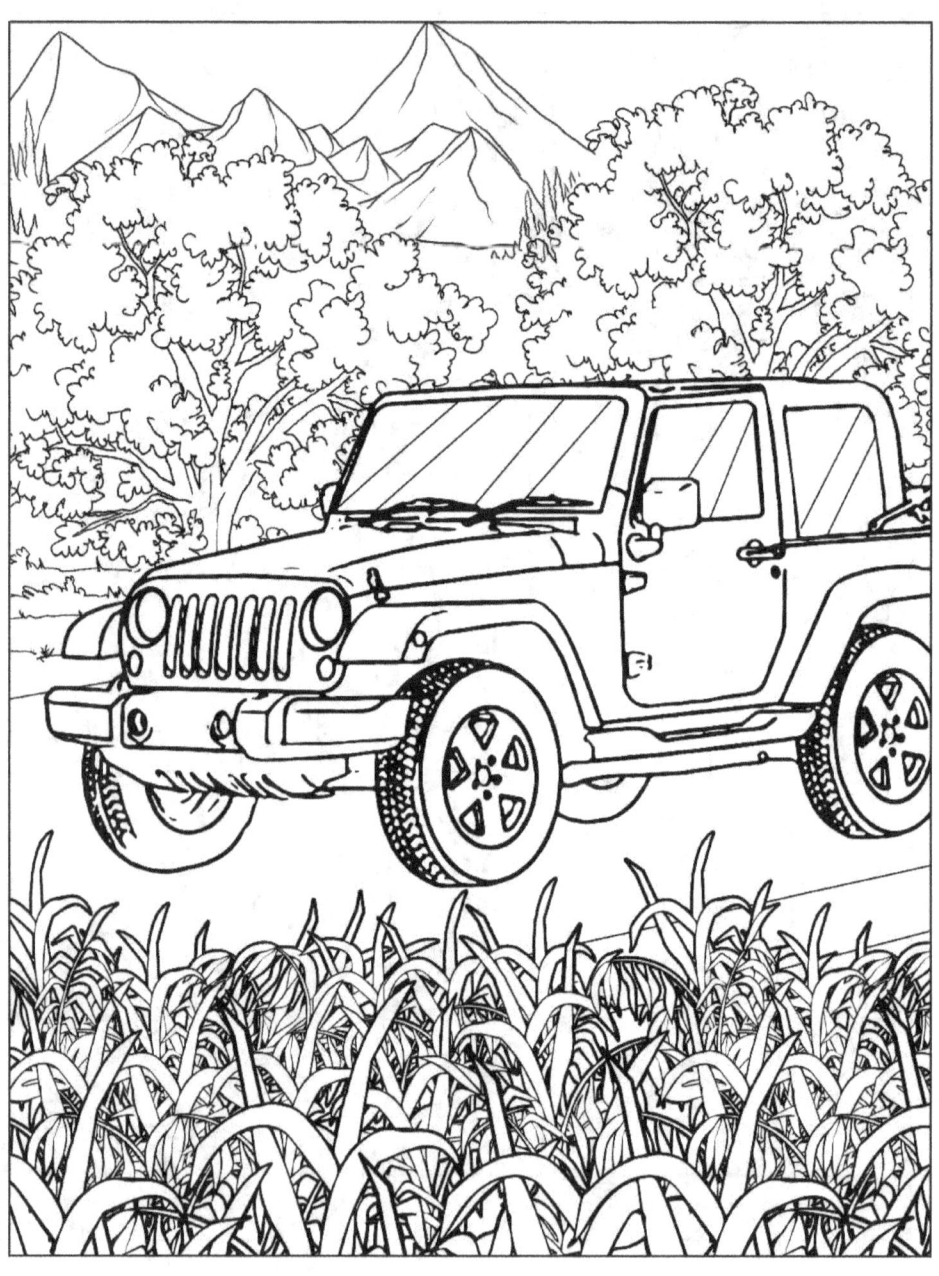

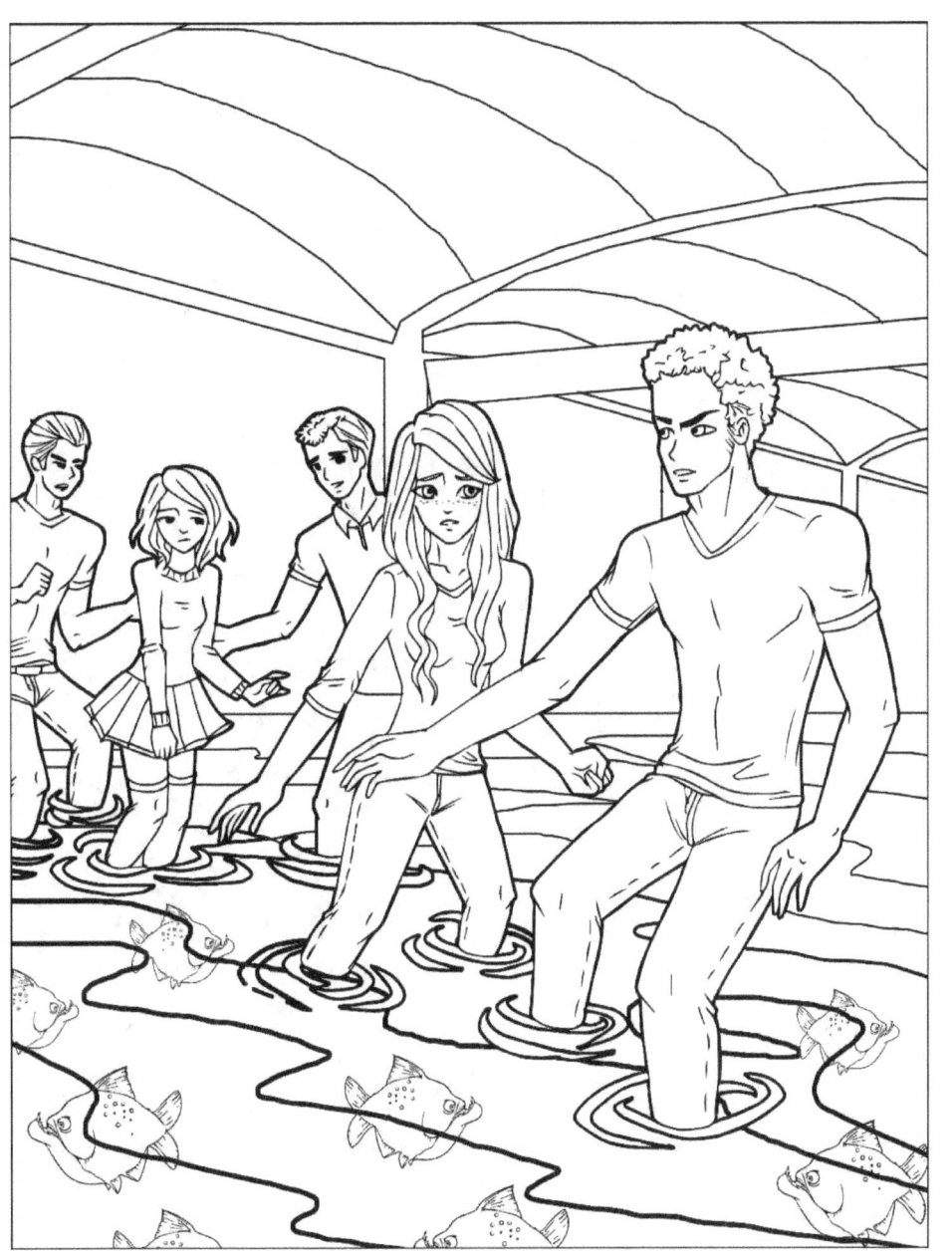

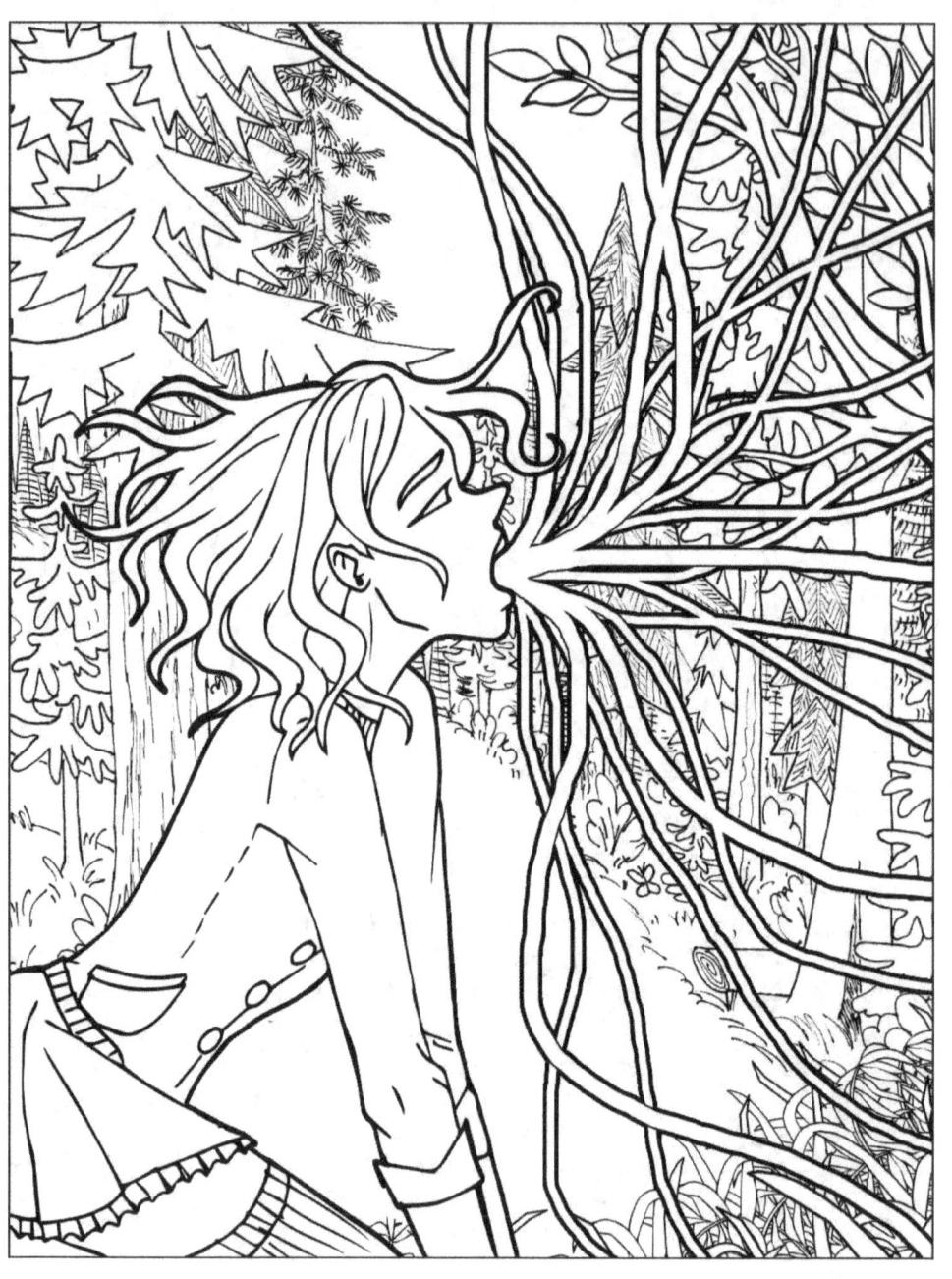

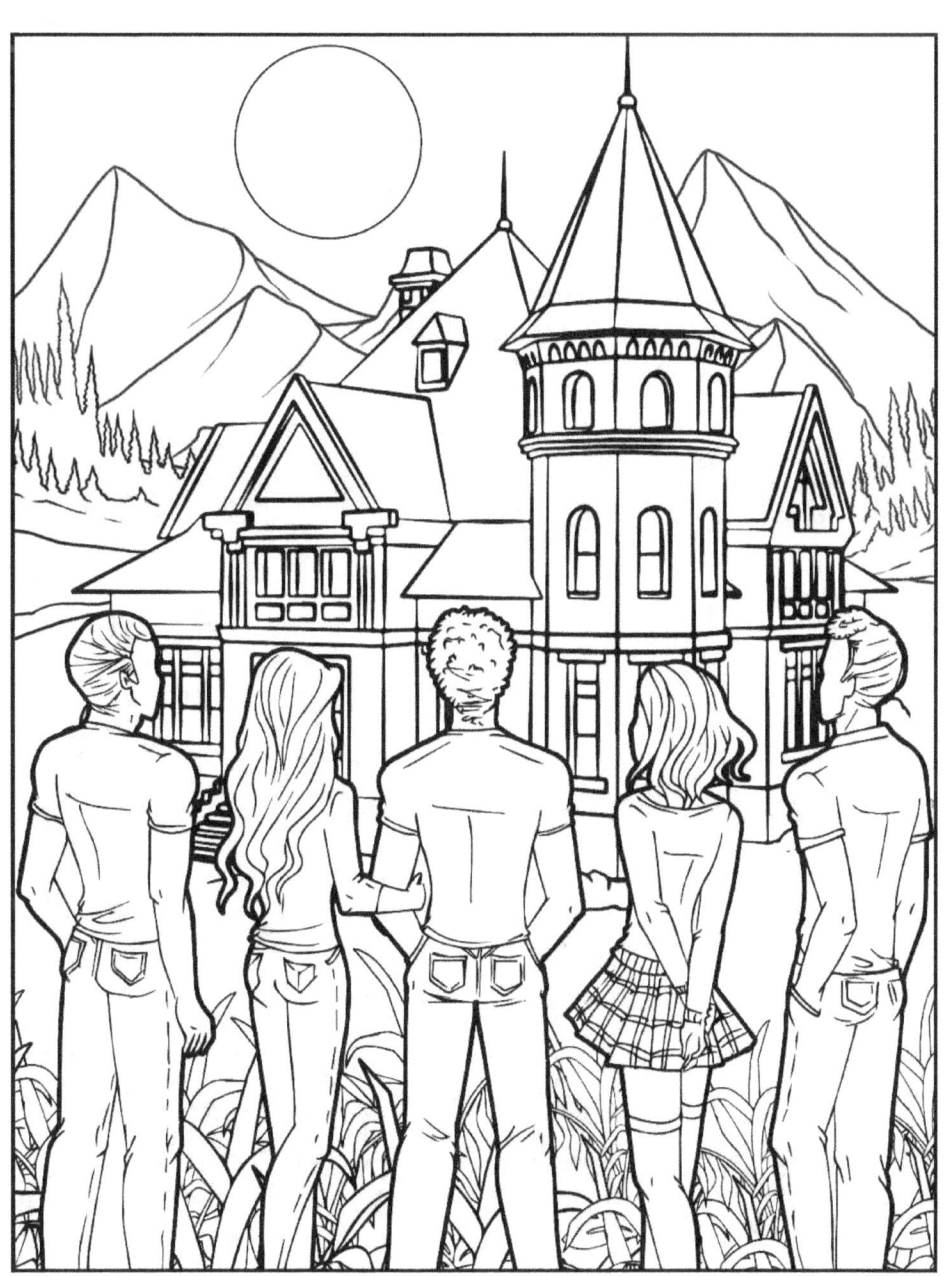

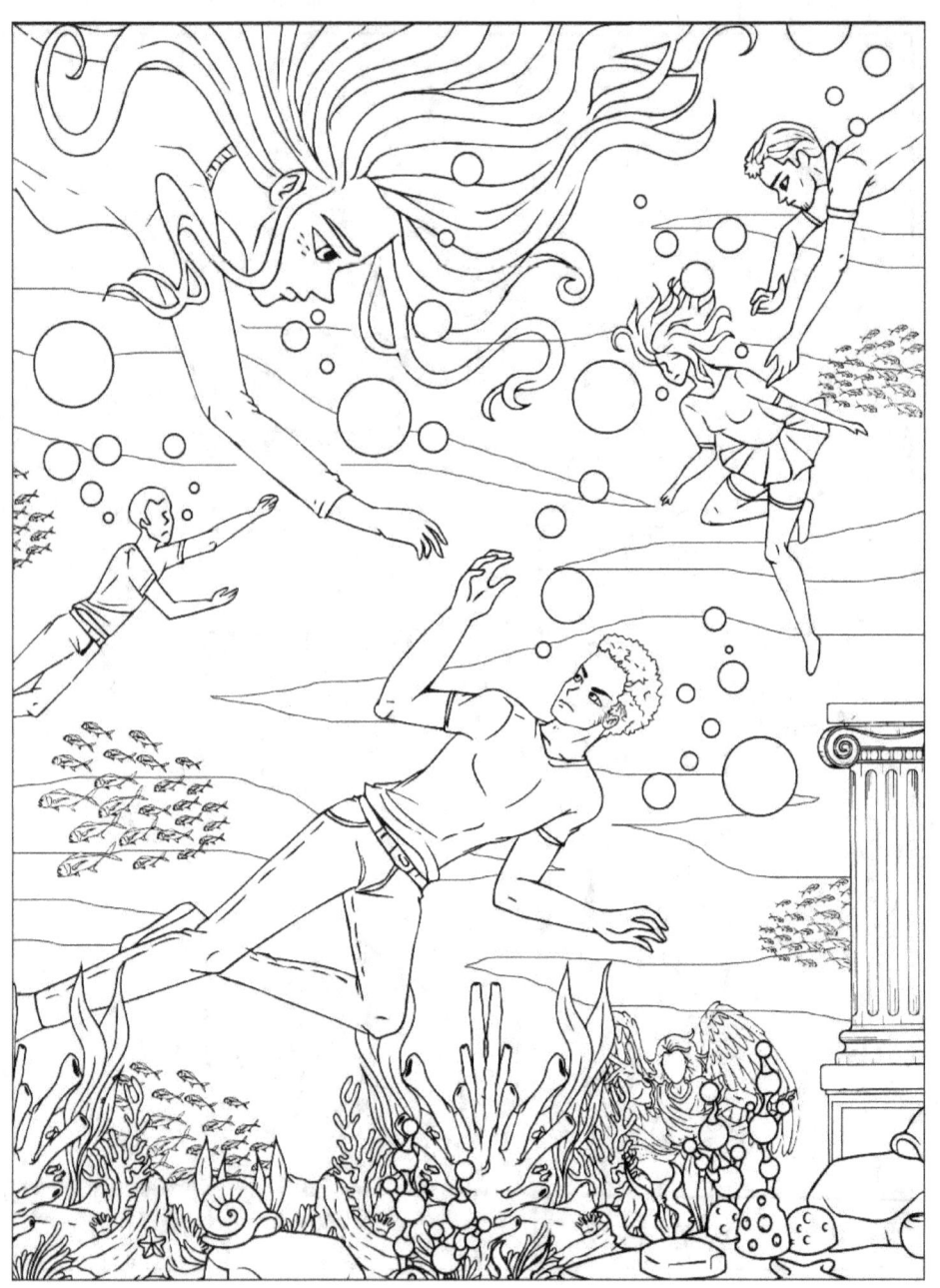

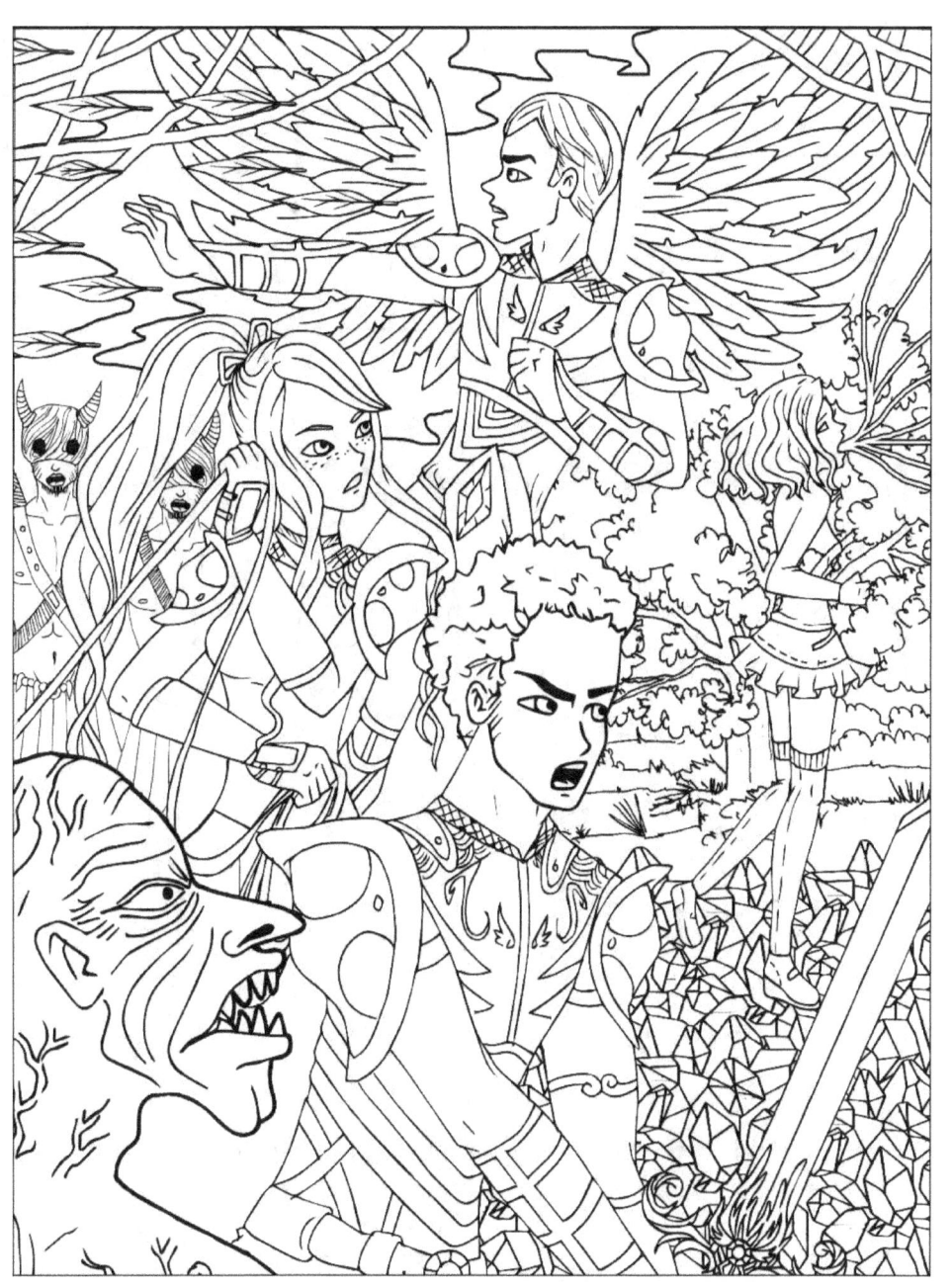

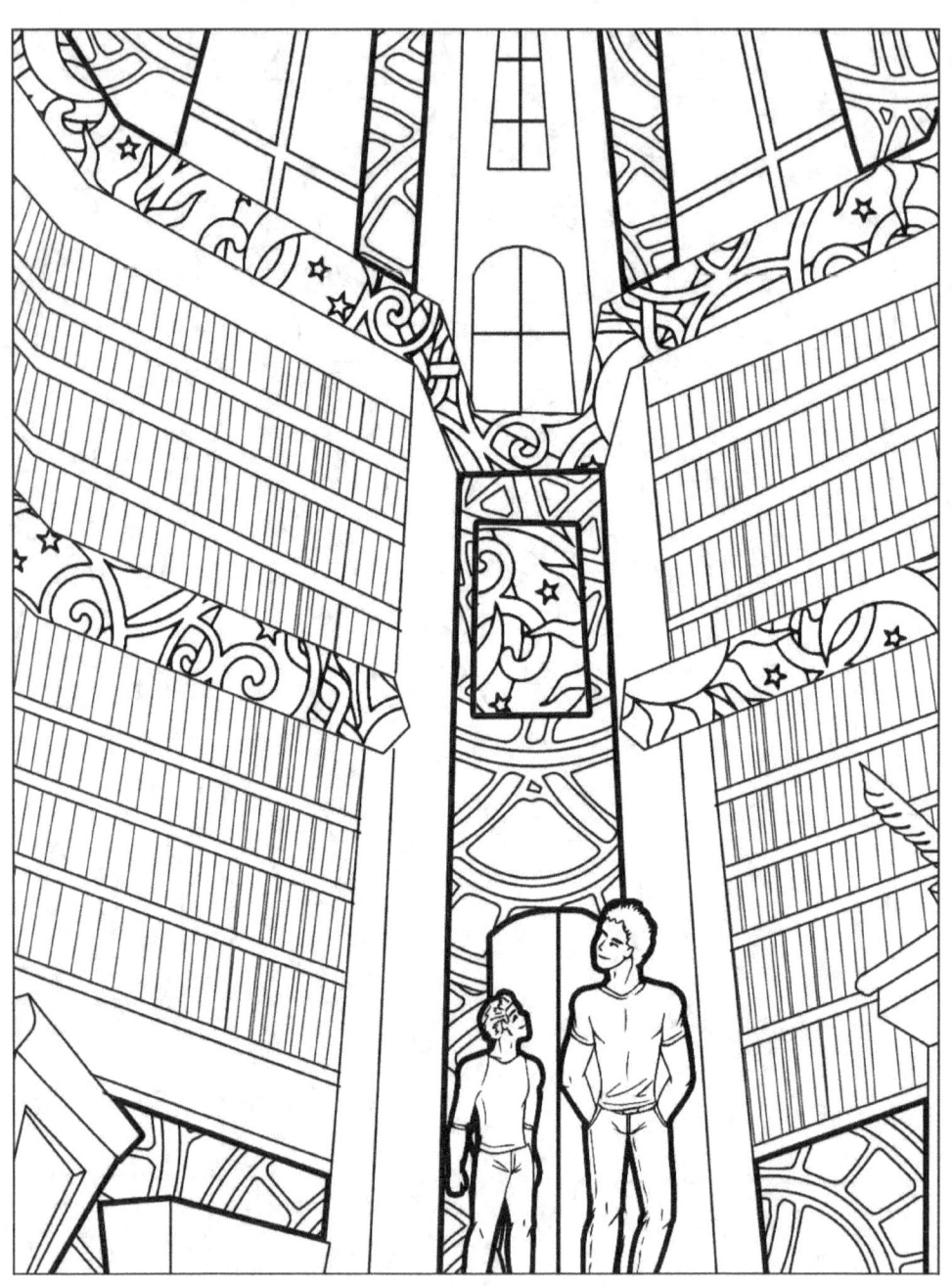

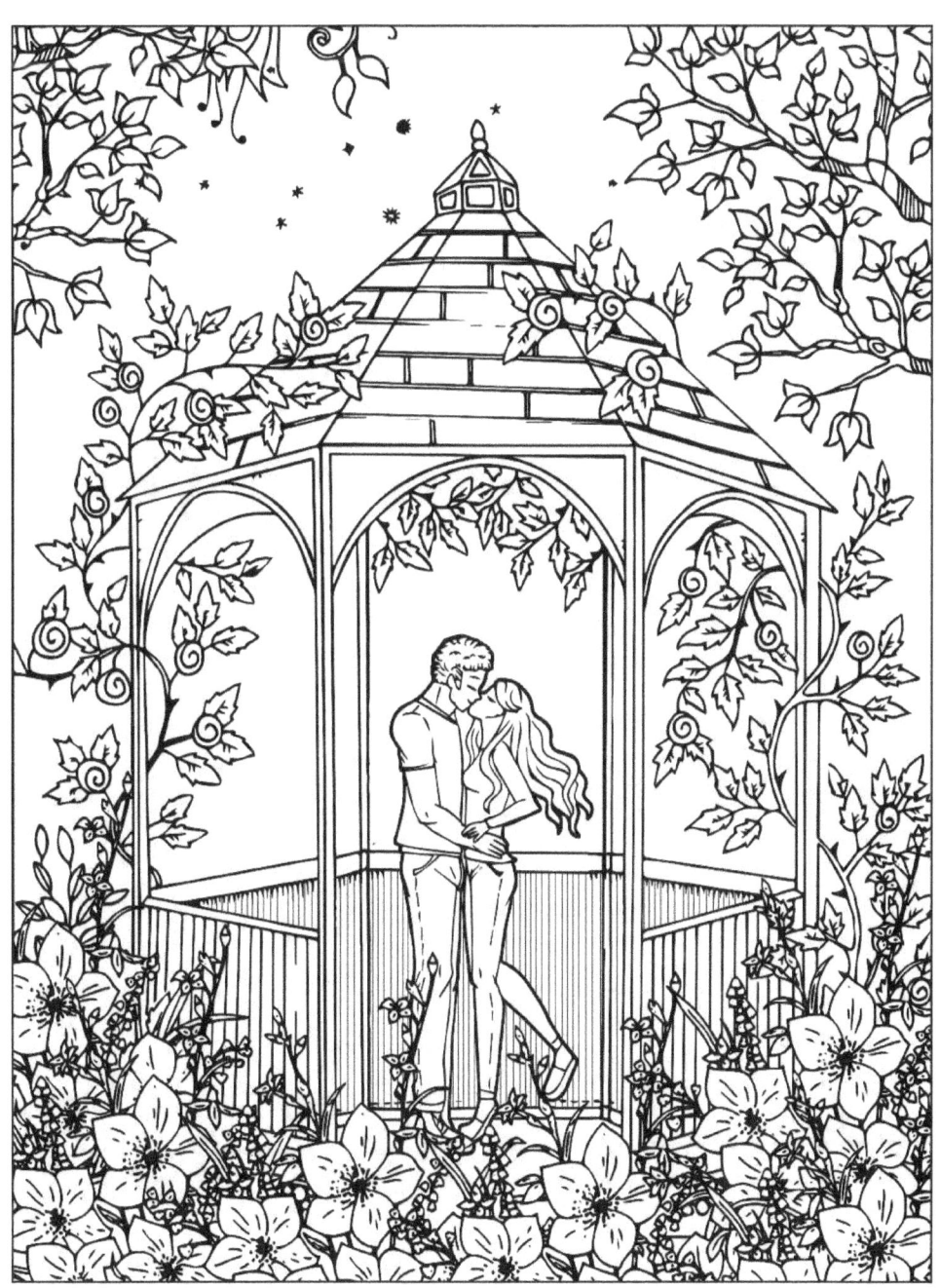

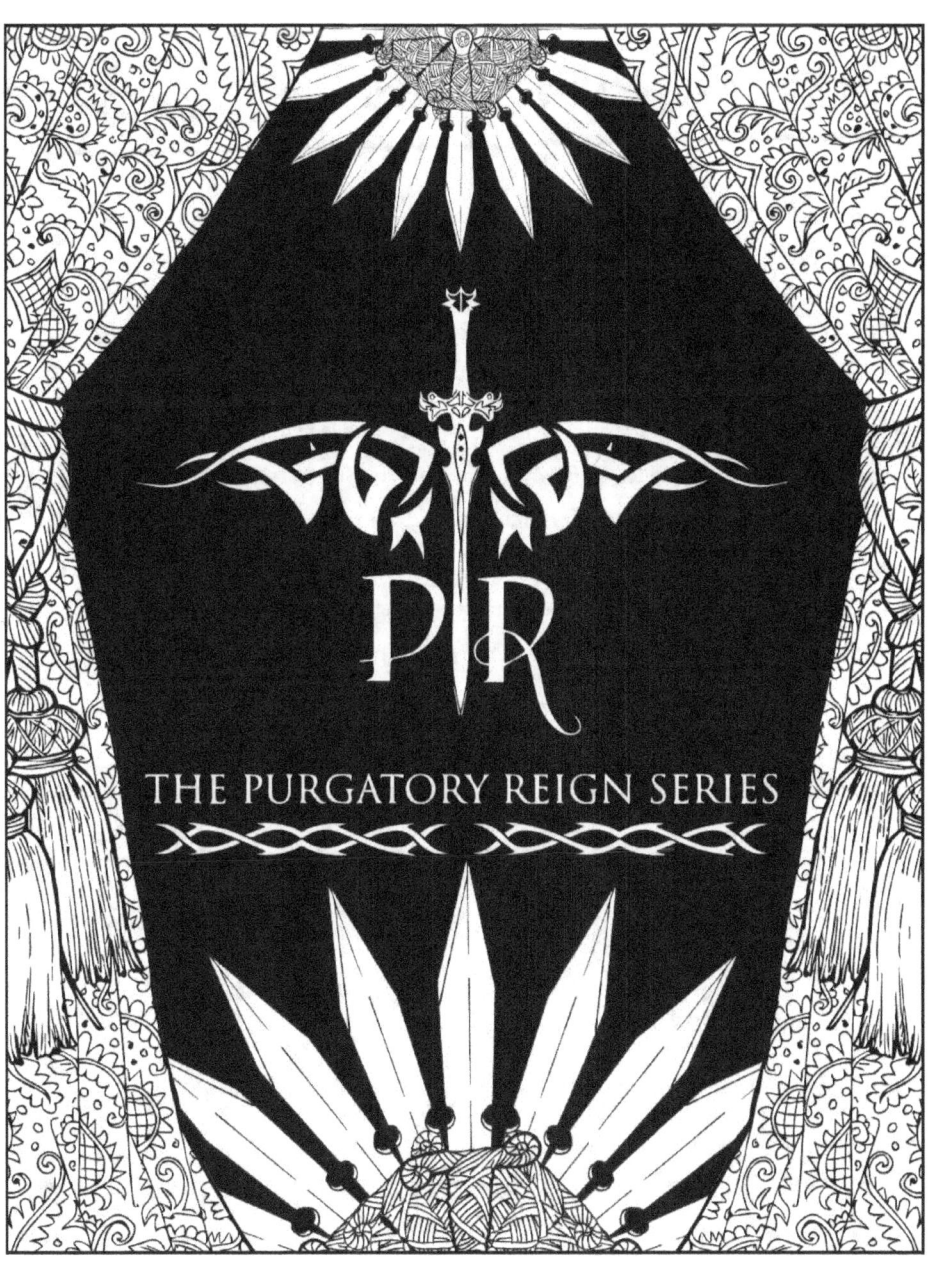

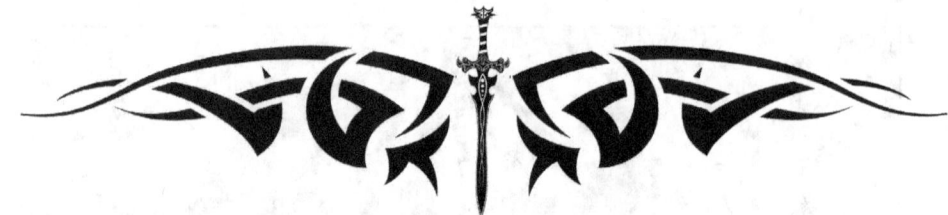

ABOUT THE AUTHOR

LM. Preston is an avid reader. She loved to create poetry and short stories as a young girl. With a thirst for knowledge she attended college and worked in the IT field as a Techie and Educator for over sixteen years. She started writing science fiction under the encouragement of her husband who was a Sci-Fi buff and her four kids. Her first published novel, Explorer X - Alpha was the beginning of her obsessive desire to write and create stories of young people who overcome unbelievable odds. She loves to write while on the porch, watching her kids play, or when she is traveling, which is another passion that encouraged her writing.

To stay updated on upcoming books, sales and new releases follow me:

Blog http://lmpreston.blogspot.com/
Facebook https://www.facebook.com/THE-PACK-by-LM-Preston-127604857259681/
Goodreads http://www.goodreads.com/author/show/3348681.L_M_Preston
Google+ https://plus.google.com/+LMPreston
Instagram https://www.instagram.com/lm_preston/
Twitter https://twitter.com/LM_Preston

www.lmpreston.com
lm.preston@yahoo.com

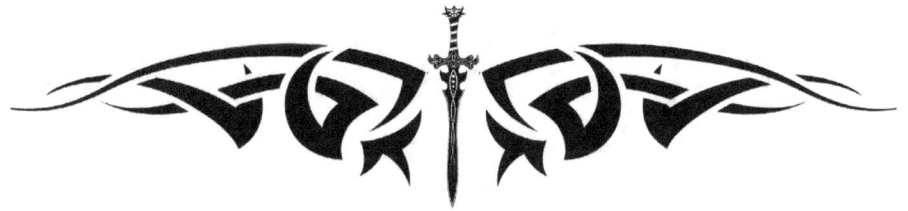

ALSO BY L.M. PRESTON

PURGATORY REIGN SERIES
Purgatory Reign, Book 1
Deviant Storm, Book 2
Fierce Tides, Book 3

THE PACK SERIES
The Pack, Book 1
Retribution, Book 2

THE BANDITS SERIES
Bandits, Book 1
Wastelands, Book 2

STANDALONES
Flutter Of Luv

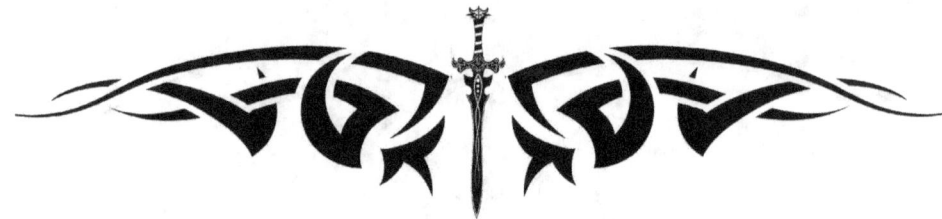

OTHER BOOKS BY LM. PRESTON

The Pack by LM Preston–

Teen, blind, vigilante on a mission to save the missing kids on mars. Shamira is considered an outcast by most, but little do they know that she is on a mission. Kids on Mars are disappearing, but Shamira decides to use the criminals' most unlikely weapons against them—the very kids who they have captured. In order to succeed, she is forced to trust another, something she is afraid to do. However, Valens, her connection to the underworld of her enemy, proves to be a useful ally. Time is slipping, and so is her control on the power that resides within her. But in order to save her brother's life, she is willing to risk it all.

Bandits by LM Preston –

Daniel's father has gotten himself killed and left another mess for Daniel to clean up. To save his world from destruction, he must fight off his father's killers while discovering a way to save his world. He wants to go it alone, but his cousin and his best friend's sister, Jade insists on tagging along. Jade is off limits to him, but she insist on changing his mind. He hasn't decided if loving her is worth the beating he'll get from her brother in order to have her. Retrieving the treasure is his only choice. But in order to get it, Daniel must choose to either walk in his father's footsteps or to re-invent himself into the one to save his world.

Wastelands – Bandits Series, by LM Preston – Daniel's doing the unthinkable. He's planning to break into a prison to prove to his dead father that he has changed, only problem is – he hasn't.

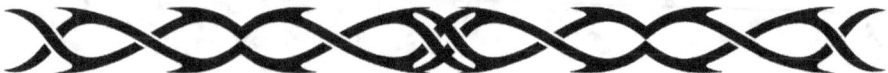

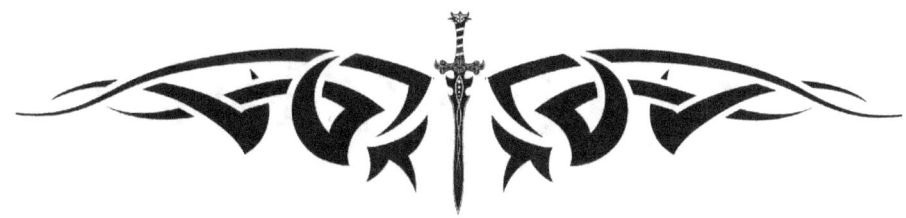

Flutter Of Luv by LM Preston—

Dawn, the neighborhood tomboy, is happy to be her best friend's shadow. Acceptance comes from playing football after school with the guys on the block while hiding safely behind her glasses, braces, and boyish ways. But Tony moves in, becomes the star running back on her school's football team, and changes her world and her view of herself forever.

Explorer X-Beta by LM Preston –

Barely escaping their captors, Aadi and Eirena are determined to save their dying friend. After their final confrontation with the species that tortured them, they've changed— unfortunately, not for the better. The changes caused by a terrible experiment force Aadi to accept the possibility that he may never be fit to go home, and that holding onto his sanity, or leading his friends to safety will end in failure and may rip his friendship with Eirena apart, forever. Time is slipping away and the possibility of losing his friend is not an option, but the foe that awaits them may be worse than the one they left.

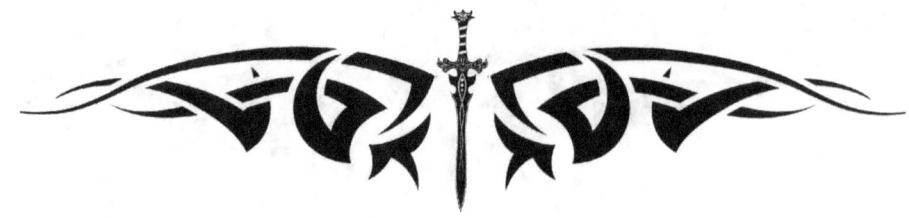

ARTIST BIO

Artist: Arnild Cuarteron Aldepolla

Arnild Cuarteron Aldepolla is a freelance artist who just can't stop drawing. He is a huge fan of young adult and teen books and can often be found doodling inspirations from anime/manga and Disney. He's the artist behind the coloring book for both teens and adult of some authors including Cameo Renae's Hidden Wings, Shelly Crane's Significance, Randi Cooley Wilson's Revelation, Ednah Walters' Runes and many more.

Arnild has a Bachelor of Fine Arts in Visual Communication from PWC, and resides in Davao City, Philippines with his mother. He is currently working on several more coloring books anticipating release next year.

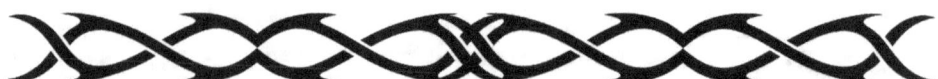

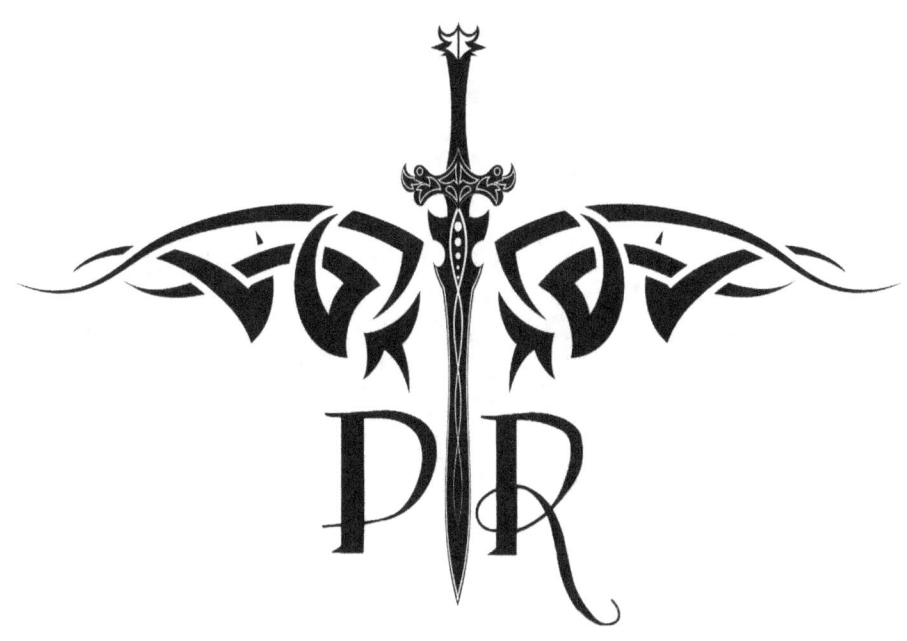

THE PURGATORY REIGN SERIES

www.ingramcontent.com/pod-product-compliance
Lightning Source LLC
Chambersburg PA
CBHW030038230526
45472CB00002B/562